Arms Control and Confidence Building in the Middle East

Contributors

W. Seth Carus was a senior fellow at the Washington Institute for Near East Policy when he worked on this project. He now works in the Office of the Secretary of Defense.

Peter D. Constable formerly headed the Multinational Force and Observers in the Sinai and is now associated with Search for Common Ground.

Richard E. Darilek is a senior staff member of the RAND Corporation.

Charles Flowerree is the former U.S. ambassador to the Conference on Disarmament.

Geoffrey Kemp is a senior associate at the Carnegie Endowment for International Peace.

Michael Krepon is the president of the Henry L. Stimson Center.

Janne E. Nolan is a senior fellow at the Brookings Institution.

Alan Platt, former senior official with the Arms Control and Disarmament Agency, is a Washington-based consultant on international and security affairs.

Brad Roberts is the editor of the *Washington Quarterly*.

Arms Control and Confidence Building in the Middle East

Alan Platt, *Editor*

Foreword by Ambassador Samuel W. Lewis

UNITED STATES
INSTITUTE OF PEACE PRESS

Washington, D.C.

United States Institute of Peace
1550 M Street, N.W.
Washington, D.C. 20005

© 1992 by the Endowment of the United States Institute of Peace. All rights reserved.

First published 1992

Printed in the United States of America

The paper used in this publication meets the minimum requirements of American National Standard for Information Sciences—Permanence of Paper for Printed Library Materials, ANSI Z39.48-1984.

Library of Congress Cataloging-in-Publication Data
Arms control and confidence building in the Middle East / edited by Alan Platt.
    p. cm.
  "March 1992."
  ISBN 1-878379-18-6
  1. Arms control—Middle East. 2. Middle East—National security.
I. Platt, Alan, 1944–
JX1974.A768835 1992   92-18784
327.1'74'0956–dc20   CIP

Contents

Foreword

There are all too many reasons why arms control experts traditionally have focused little attention on the Middle East. Perhaps the most important is that the political terrain has seemed so unpromising. Yet this region remains unstable, afflicted with multiple conflicts that remain unpredictably explosive at best, and a ready market for the inflow of increasingly sophisticated weapon technologies. The 1991 Persian Gulf War and the widespread introduction of ballistic missiles and chemical weapons into the region only underscore this point.

Recognizing that the time was ripe for a new look at an old problem, the Henry L. Stimson Center initiated a project that brought together a number of arms control experts whose work has concentrated primarily on Europe. By refocusing their attention on the Middle East region, the project could draw on lessons learned from the East-West conflict during the Cold War. To situate the analysis within the political realities of the Middle East, the project director, Alan Platt, arranged for each chapter in this volume to be coauthored by a Middle East expert. This book is the result of that unusual cross-fertilization. The project was supported by a grant from the United States Institute of Peace as well as by funding from other sources.

This publication is one product of a much larger effort by the Institute to contribute through research, education, and public information to a more peaceful and durable order in the Middle East. In early spring 1991, the Institute established its Special Middle East Program in Peacemaking and Conflict Resolution to initiate several new project activities that complement the expanded priority being accorded to Middle Eastern topics within the Institute's ongoing grant, fellowship, and in-house research programs. One initial activity was the convening in early 1991 of an expert study group to debate many of the arms control issues treated in this volume. Most of the authors participated in that group. A short report based on its initial sessions was widely disseminated in May 1991 to policymakers, the Congress, and the public.

This is the first book resulting from an Institute grant to be published by the USIP Press. It provides further evidence of the Institute's continuing effort to inform discussion and debate on how to counter regional and international conflicts in ways that will lead to a more peaceful world.

Samuel W. Lewis, President
United States Institute of Peace

Acknowledgments

I am grateful to the United States Institute of Peace for providing the bulk of financial support that has made this volume possible. I also wish to thank the Henry L. Stimson Center (a nonprofit, nonpartisan institution devoted to public policy research), the Carnegie Corporation of New York, the W. Alton Jones Foundation, and the Rockefeller Brothers Fund for their support. Finally, I want to thank in particular Michael Krepon, president of the Stimson Center, who has provided encouragement and wise counsel throughout this project. Of course, the opinions, findings, and conclusions or recommendations expressed in this publication are those of the authors and do not necessarily reflect the views of the Institute or any other organization.

Alan Platt

Abbreviations

ABM	Anti-Ballistic Missile
ACDA	Arms Control and Disarmament Agency
CBM	Confidence-building measure
CD	Conference on Disarmament
CFE	Conventional Forces in Europe
CPC	Conflict Prevention Center
CSBM	Confidence- and security-building measure
CSCE	Conference on Security and Cooperation in Europe
CWC	Chemical Weapons Convention
FBIS	Foreign Broadcast Information Service
IAEA	International Atomic Energy Agency
INF	Intermediate-range Nuclear Forces
MBFR	Mutual and Balanced Force Reduction
MFO	Multinational Force and Observers
NATO	North Atlantic Treaty Organization
NPT	Nuclear Non-Proliferation Treaty
NTM	National technical means
OSI	On-site inspection
SALT	Strategic Arms Limitation Talks
START	Strategic Arms Reduction Talks
UNDOF	UN Disengagement Observer Force
UNIFIL	UN Interim Force in Lebanon
UNIMOG	UN Iran-Iraq Military Observer Group

Chronology

1958   Surprise Attack Conference held in Geneva

1962   Cuban Missile Crisis
Eighteen Nation Disarmament Committee meets

1963   Washington and Moscow agree to set up hot line and to
ban nuclear testing in the atmosphere

1963–67   Yemen Civil War

1967   Six Day War

1968   NPT signed

1968–70   War of Attrition

1969–72   SALT I

1971   Agreement on Measures to Reduce the Risk of Outbreak
of Nuclear War signed

1972   ABM Treaty signed
Incidents at Sea Agreement signed
Biological Weapons Convention signed

1973   Agreement on the Prevention of Nuclear War signed
Negotiations begin in Vienna to reduce both NATO and
Warsaw Pact conventional force structures in central
Europe
October War between Egypt and Israel

1974   Israel and Syria agree to on-site challenge inspections of
        their forces in the Golan Heights by the United Nations
        Nine Canadians killed when UN aircraft shot down by
        Syria
        Vladivostok Accords signed

1975   UN aerial photographic coverage of the Sinai extended
        indefinitely
        Helsinki Final Act of the CSCE signed

1976   Syria and Israel agree to red-line agreement concerning
        Lebanon

1977   Anwar Sadat visits Jerusalem

1979   Egyptian-Israeli peace treaty signed
        SALT II Treaty signed
        Soviet Union invades Afghanistan

1980   Iran-Iraq War breaks out

1984   Facsimile transmission capability added to U.S.-Soviet
        hot line

1986   U.S.-Soviet INF Treaty signed
        Stockholm Document on Confidence- and Security-
        Building Measures signed

1987   Agreement signed to establish nuclear risk reduction
        centers in Washington and Moscow
        Missile Technology Control Regime established

1988   Iraq admits to using chemical weapons in Iran
        Presumed chemical weapons plant discovered in Rabta,
        Libya

1989   CSBM talks begin in Vienna
        Negotiations on CFE begin
        Gorbachev's UN speech emphasizes East-West arms control
        Canberra Government-Industry Conference against
        Chemical Weapons

1990   CFE treaty produced
       Vienna Document on CSBMs signed
       Charter of Paris agreed to
       Iraq invades Kuwait

1991   Persian Gulf War
       Australia Group agrees on list of chemical weapons pre-
           cursors to come under export control
       Bush and Gorbachev propose initiative for elimination
           of short-range nuclear forces
       Big Five arms suppliers meet in Paris and London to dis-
           cuss arms sales policies
       Middle East peace talks begin in Madrid

1992   U.S. Senate ratifies CFE treaty
       Open Skies Treaty signed
       Big Five arms suppliers meet in Washington
       START treaty concluded
       Multilateral talks on Middle East regional issues, includ-
           ing arms control, begin

1. Introduction

Alan Platt

Notwithstanding recent peace talks among the countries of the Middle East, foreign policy analysts—inside and outside the U.S. government—continue to be concerned about the possible outbreak of hostilities in this volatile region. Part of this concern is fueled by the perception that the nations of this region have historically pursued their security interests by expanding and modernizing their military forces and periodically using them to achieve their policy ends. This concern is further exacerbated by the fact that the nations of the Middle East have historically exhibited little interest in arms control or reaching political compromises that mutually constrain military capabilities.

Yet, the potential causes of instability in the Middle East are growing. Although the eight-year Iran-Iraq War and the Persian Gulf War are now over, hostile feelings remain and a number of countries in the region are perceptibly fearful about their future security. Arab-Israeli tensions remain in the absence of tangible progress toward a diplomatic settlement of the central issues in dispute. At the same time, sophisticated new conventional arms are being transferred into the region. By the middle of 1992, the United States alone had agreed to transfer to the region more than $20 billion of advanced conventional arms since the end of the Persian Gulf War. And in the past few years a number of countries in the region have reportedly acquired surface-to-surface missiles, chemical weapons, and biological weapons, and are rapidly increasing their ability to produce these weapons indigenously and to deploy them clandestinely.

Unchecked, these developments are likely to intensify in coming years as traditional as well as new Third World arms suppliers (such as Argentina, Brazil, and India) expand their arms-exporting capabilities and as more Middle Eastern countries seek to modernize their conventional and unconventional weapons arsenals. A number of these developments—such as the coupling of chemical weapons and ballistic missile arsenals in the region and the possible "brain drain" of Russian scientists to the Middle East—have potentially ominous implications for Middle Eastern states as well as U.S. security interests there. Although no causal relationship between inventories of arms and the likelihood of war exists, there is little question but that many of these developments will heighten tensions and ensure that any future conflict in the Middle East will be devastating.

This project was initiated in the belief that with the end of the Cold War—and subsequently the Persian Gulf War—it was a propitious time to take a fresh look at the possibilities for arms control in the Middle East. For this project, arms control was broadly conceived as "any measure that reduces the likelihood of war as an instrument of policy or that limits the destructiveness and duration of war should it break out."[1] The underlying premise of the project was that various postwar East-West arms control efforts provide a number of lessons—some positive and some negative—for the possible role of arms control in the Middle East and that these lessons are important to identify and evaluate for their future relevance to the Middle East in particular and the Third World in general.

Accordingly, several papers were commissioned to look at different possible approaches to arms control in the Middle East. For each paper, one coauthor was chosen for his or her detailed knowledge of a particular arms control approach that was developed in an East-West context. The other coauthor was chosen because of extensive experience in the Middle East region.

Each chapter in this volume concludes, in its own way, that the current possibilities for arms control in the Middle East are limited. Implicit in each chapter is the understanding that in the absence of substantial movement in the peace process, there are serious limitations on what is likely to be achieved in the area of arms control. Although the ongoing peace talks have been important for bringing Israelis and Arabs together for face-to-face meetings, these talks have not achieved (at least by spring 1992) what the Bush administration had hoped for—a substantive breakthrough based on a transformation in the attitudes of the countries in the region. Nevertheless, all the chapters argue that there are some interesting near-term possibilities for arms control in the Middle East, particularly concerning confidence- and security-building measures (CSBMs), and that these efforts should be explored in parallel with the peace process and not be held hostage to achieving substantial progress in the formal peace negotiations.

In an article published in 1987, Richard Darilek of the RAND Corporation and a contributor to this volume, drew an important distinction between structural and operational arms control.[2] Darilek argued that two different approaches to arms control were pursued in East-West arms control efforts during the 1970s and 1980s. One effort, which he termed the "structural" approach, centered around Vienna. There, NATO and Warsaw Pact countries engaged in formal arms control negotiations—first the Mutual and Balanced Force Reduction (MBFR) Talks and later the Conventional Forces in Europe (CFE) negotiations. These talks to scale down the two blocs' manpower and military equipment ultimately produced agreement to make major reductions in NATO and Warsaw Pact forces. A second arms control effort was carried out in the context of the Conference on Security and Cooperation in Europe (CSCE). These talks focused on CSBMs rather than on reducing the size of the forces of the participating NATO, Warsaw Pact, and neutral countries, and, as such, were characterized by Darilek as "operational" arms control.

Beginning with the Helsinki Final Act of 1975, the operational approach led to the 1986 "Document of the Stockholm Conference on Confidence- and Security-Building Measures," wherein CSBMs were defined as "arrangements designed to enhance assurance of mind and belief in the trustworthiness of states and the facts they create."[3] The Stockholm Document and the follow-on 1990 Vienna Document laid out various agreed-upon procedures governing NATO and Warsaw Pact countries' military activities in Europe—the exchange of certain information, the provision of advance notifications of exercises or concentrations of troops in excess of various thresholds, the invitation of observers to such activities, and the establishment of procedures for inspections of questionable activities, among other things.

Although these measures are likely to be difficult to achieve in the Middle East in the near term (it was eleven years from the signing of the Helsinki Final Act to the conclusion of the Stockholm Document), CSBMs are likely, for the foreseeable future, to have more relevance and utility in the Middle East than structural arms control efforts. As Darilek and Kemp observe in their chapter on CSBMs in the Middle East, arms control efforts in this region need to start with preliminary or "precursor" CSBMs, not structural arms control efforts or even sophisticated Stockholm-type CSBMs, to begin to bridge centuries of hostilities and the consequent lack of communication among the countries of the Middle East. Focusing on the kinds of information exchange measures agreed to early in the East-West context, Darilek and Kemp recommend for the Middle East such precursor CSBMs as holding informal seminars about military doctrine and setting up communications hot lines. Such measures, by increasing transparency and mutual understanding, could help reduce the risk of war. Obversely, in the absence of any precursor CSBMs, various military activities in the Middle East could be miscalculated and serve as a catalyst to inadvertent war, that is, a war that neither side wanted nor expected at the outset of a crisis.

Each of the other chapters in this volume reaches the same conclusion as Darilek and Kemp: arms control in the Middle East should begin with modest CSBMs, building on past experiences in the region and taking into account what is feasible in political terms. Krepon and Constable argue in their chapter, for example, that the successful 1974 Israeli-Syrian disengagement agreement on the Golan Heights and the 1979 Sinai demilitarization accord between Israel and Egypt suggest that aerial inspections might be used for future confidence building among the parties of the Middle East. Carus and Nolan argue that any missile restraint efforts in the Middle East should focus initially on such CSBMs as information and intelligence exchanges, prior notification of missile tests, and limited visits to defense production and space launch facilities. Finally, Flowerree and Roberts argue that chemical weapons arms control efforts in the Middle East could most usefully be pursued in the near term by focusing on the kinds of transparency measures that gained broad support in the international negotiations held in Geneva to conclude the Chemical Weapons Convention (CWC).

In all the chapters, the common assumption is that formal structural East-West arms control negotiating approaches, such as the MBFR, strategic arms limitation talks, and strategic arms reduction talks, are not likely to bear fruit any time soon in the Middle East. Initial efforts involving regional participants, if they are to be successful, need to begin with relatively noncontroversial measures to build confidence and improve communications among the parties of the region. Such measures—precursor CSBMs—are likely to hold the greatest chance for success if they are introduced in a step-by-step manner and build on previous successful efforts in the region.

For these types of precursor CSBMs to succeed, at least two basic preconditions are required: the measures must not directly undermine the security of the regional parties and they must be acceptable to all participating states. These two preconditions can be met, it is argued in this volume, if the CSBMs are not too ambitious to begin with and are formulated in a manner that takes into account the historical experiences and interests of the countries in the region. Although the lack of diplomatic recognition between Israel and all but one of its Arab neighbors constitutes a potentially serious roadblock to far-reaching CSBMs, it need not bar new steps. Some precursor CSBMs, however, may have to be tacit rather than formal and carried out through the good offices of third parties.

This step-by-step approach was how arms control was, in fact, effectively pursued by the United States and the Soviet Union during most of the postwar era when serious political differences divided the two nuclear superpowers. In this light, the pursuit of arms control in the Middle East today can most usefully be compared with the pursuit of arms control between the superpowers during the 1960s, not the 1990s. Indeed, arms control typically makes the most sense between adversaries who, despite all their antagonisms, share certain common interests. Even the most hostile states can find common ground, for example, in the types of CSBMs that help prevent accidental wars and unintended escalation.

Taken together, the collaborative chapters that follow should be seen as part of a larger process to develop the intellectual infrastructure for arms control in the Middle East. These ideas may not be appropriate for immediate negotiation and implementation, but they can be "stockpiled" for future application in the region. If the suitability of a particular approach to a problem appears highly limited in 1992, we should not forget that even the idea of holding Middle East peace talks among the regions' participants was extremely unlikely before the Persian Gulf War. It is also worth recalling that the body of literature on East-West arms control that was developed during the 1960s and 1970s was not translated into policy until many years later.

In short, this volume was put together with the understanding that the current applicability of arms control in the Middle East would likely be limited and, in any case, arms control could not solve the long-standing rivalries and differences among the nations of the region. The key issues in dispute ultimately must be resolved through negotiation, and failure to progress in the peace process will inevitably limit arms control in the region. Nevertheless, the time is ripe to begin developing a body of analytical literature on the pros and cons of particular approaches to arms control in the Middle East, utilizing the skills and experience of experts in Middle Eastern affairs as well as practitioners and scholars of East-West arms control efforts. Progress on the Middle East arms control front may not go very far or very fast for lack of political will at this time but it is implicit in this volume that progress should not be held back by a lack of useful arms control ideas, especially ideas aimed at building confidence and reducing tensions in the region.

If we set modest goals for initial Middle East arms control efforts, if we try to pursue these efforts on a step-by-step basis, if we truly put America's post–Persian Gulf War prestige behind initial acceptance of precursor CSBMs among the countries of the Middle East, if we try to take into account the security concerns of all the different nations of the region, and if we make this effort a consistently high-priority item on our foreign policy agenda, the United States can succeed in helping to build confidence and promote arms control in the region. Indeed, under these circumstances, a considerably wider range of policy instruments to promote peace in the Middle East is likely to be available than if international efforts concentrate on either formal peace negotiations or structural efforts to reduce the size of the arsenals in the region.

2. Prospects for Confidence- and Security-Building Measures in the Middle East

Richard E. Darilek and Geoffrey Kemp

This chapter begins by reviewing the record of arms control developments related to confidence- and security-building measures (CSBMs) in Europe during the Cold War. Such a review establishes at the outset a baseline understanding of both established practice and evolving theory of one concrete, highly prominent, and presumably successful case of CSBMs being applied to real-world security problems. The chapter then attempts to extrapolate from the European experience and explore the potential contributions that CSBMs might make to stability and security in the Middle East. In its presentation of the issues involved, the chapter pays particular attention to the dissimilarities, as well as the potential congruities, between security problems that occurred in Europe during the Cold War and those currently confronting the Middle East.

Vast differences exist between Europe and the Middle East, to be sure. Nowhere are these differences more apparent than in the realm of security. In Europe, for example, a general consensus exists on where geographic boundaries of the region and where territorial borders of states within the region should be. Furthermore, there is general—even formal—agreement in Europe that war is an illegitimate instrument of policy when it comes to changing borders. Such an agreement was one of the outcomes of World War II. It survived the tensions of the Cold War era to become one of the pillars of the new security order that is emerging in Europe.

The Middle East, however, is still ill-defined—whether as a geographic region or as a collection of individual states with mutually recognized territorial boundaries. While Europe can be characterized by the consensus it has reached on certain basic security issues, the Middle East is conspicuous for its lack of consensus on such issues. War, for example, is still a viable policy instrument for many countries in the Middle East. In particular, war is considered an acceptable means for changing territorial borders—an overarching security issue on which precious little agreement exists in the Middle East.

Nevertheless, it can be argued that for most countries in regions of the world such as the Middle East, where international crisis and conflict loom as distinct possibilities, the range of security problems being confronted is not totally dissimilar from the problems faced in Europe during the Cold War years. In addition to problems involving fundamental issues of peace and war, many of the security problems encountered in the Middle East raise other basic issues such as a country's rights to territorial integrity, secure borders, and international recognition of statehood. During the Cold War, Europe developed a variety of useful approaches to security problems. Arms control efforts in general and CSBMs in particular were prominent among these approaches. Potentially, these efforts could contribute to security in the Middle East as well. Before that can be established, however, it is necessary to obtain a more specific understanding of the types of CSBMs that have been developed thus far. For this understanding, one can look to Europe, where such measures, at least in their postwar incarnation, were born and bred.

A Brief History

What we now call confidence-building measures (CBMs) probably owe their origins, at least in part, to the European military practice of inviting observers from various states to military exercises. This practice dates back to before World War I, if not much earlier. Similar measures emerged after that war in the context of the Versailles Treaty's attempt to control a defeated Germany.[1] Among other things, that treaty provided for the demilitarization of the Rhineland (a type of constraint) and on-site inspections (OSIs) announced six days in advance (an access measure).

Precursor CSBMs

Following World War II, military liaison missions between and among the four victorious allied powers were established, ostensibly to improve relationships (build confidence) among the forces of those allies occupying Germany. With the onset of the Cold War, these missions soon turned into military intelligence-gathering devices (access measures) for all parties involved. In the 1950s and 1960s, forerunners of modern CSBMs were proposed at the Surprise Attack Conference held in Geneva in 1958 and to the Eighteen Nation Disarmament Committee in 1962.[2] Two U.S. proposals during this period were actually instituted in the form of the hot line's direct communication links between national command authorities in Washington and Moscow (a communications CSBM) and the agreement to ban nuclear testing in the atmosphere (a constraint measure), both of which were agreed to in 1963.

The timing of these two agreements is particularly interesting: They were proposed and consummated in the immediate aftermath of the Cuban Missile Crisis. Although the Cold War was far from over, that crisis had brought it to a head both militarily and politically. By forcing the two opposing sides to confront the reality of how close they had actually come to nuclear war, the crisis, once it began to deescalate militarily, gave rise to a political climate in which new approaches to both superpower and East-West relationships were encouraged In a sense, the Cuban Missile Crisis and its aftermath fostered a welcome respite from habitual Cold War tensions and, thus, created the necessary political preconditions for arms control as we now know it. These conditions endured and even improved throughout the remainder of the 1960s. They helped give rise to the period of détente in East-West relations that characterized much of the next decade.

The first half of the 1970s witnessed a period of considerable, if short-lived, progress in both strategic nuclear and conventional arms control efforts. The first Strategic Arms Limitation Talks (SALT I) and the Anti-Ballistic Missile (ABM) Treaty in the early 1970s were followed by the Vladivostok Agreement in 1974, which raised expectations that yet another strategic arms limitation treaty (SALT II) would be concluded before the end of the decade. Fueling further expectations of progress in arms control, the United States and the Soviet Union signed, in steady succession, an Agreement on Measures to Reduce the Risk of Outbreak of Nuclear War in 1971, which provides for immediate notification of an accidental, unauthorized, or unexplained nuclear detonation; the Incidents at Sea Agreement of 1972, which establishes operating procedures to decrease potential ship-to-ship harassment (e.g., simulated attacks) during peacetime; and, in 1973, a declaratory Agreement on the Prevention of Nuclear War, which provides for immediate and urgent consultations in times of crisis.

In 1973, moreover, negotiations aimed at reducing both NATO and Warsaw Pact conventional force structures in central Europe commenced in Vienna, while preparations were well underway for a new Conference on Security and Cooperation in Europe (CSCE) with participation by all European states (except Albania) plus the United States and Canada. This period marked a Cold War high point for détente in East-West and

U.S.-Soviet relations. Political breakthroughs were also being scored through the policies of *Ostpolitik* in West Germany and their tangible results: the Quadripartite Agreement on Berlin, the rapprochement between East and West Germany, and the treaties signed by the latter with various Warsaw Pact countries (e.g., Poland), which acknowledged post–World War II borders that had been in existence at that point for over twenty-five years.

Meanwhile, in the Middle East itself following the October War of 1973, Egypt and Israel accepted the application of several CBMs in the Sinai Peninsula pursuant to their cease-fire agreement of November 1973. These measures included the creation of limited-force zones, inspections by UN forces, and air reconnaissance by U.S. aircraft. By 1974 Israel and Syria had agreed, without negotiating directly with each other, to on-site challenge inspections of their forces in the Golan Heights by the UN. The Camp David Peace Treaty of 1979 between Israel and Egypt went further in the Sinai by providing for the United States, as a third party to the agreement, to manage or conduct air reconnaissance missions; manned and unmanned observation and detection posts; early warning stations in designated (especially strategic) areas; ground, naval, and aerial patrols; and OSIs, both routine and challenge.[3]

First-Generation CBMs

The CSCE, whose first set of meetings culminated in the signing of the Helsinki Final Act in 1975, presided over the birth of the first generation of true CBMs. They were designed primarily for conventional forces in Europe. However, their arrival on the international scene was not genuinely welcomed by the superpowers, who placed whatever real hopes they might have had for conventional arms control in Europe on the Mutual and Balanced Force Reduction (MBFR) negotiations in Vienna.[4] Instead, CBMs were the favored child of neutral and nonaligned European states. These states resented their exclusion from the alliance-oriented Vienna negotiations and insisted on inserting something more than declarations of principles into the "security" component of the CSCE.

The result of these and other international interests and negotiating pressures was the "Document on Confidence Building Measures" in the Helsinki Final Act of 1975. That document contained a variety of CBMs involving:

- notification in advance (twenty-one days) of
  —major military maneuvers (more than 25,000 troops),
  —other maneuvers (less than 25,000 troops), and
  —major military movements (undefined); and
- invitation of observers to major military maneuvers.

The provision to invite observers was discretionary on the part of the state conducting the maneuvers; its inclusion represented a nod, at least, in the direction of access measures. Otherwise, given the predominance of the notification provisions in the document, this package of CBMs was heavily weighted toward producing various exchanges of information in advance of planned military activities.

The theory behind these measures was not the one associated with contemporary arms control efforts such as MBFR. Throughout the 1970s, in fact, the United States consistently refused to consider CBMs in the general category of arms control. The purpose of CBMs was not to limit the capabilities of, or otherwise control, the military forces that states had in being, it was argued, much less reduce their numbers. Nor were any verification provisions attached to these measures. Instead, as indicated in the Helsinki Final Act and elsewhere, CBMs were aimed at increasing "openness," reducing the secrecy with which military matters were traditionally surrounded (particularly in eastern Europe), and improving the predictability of military activities in general.

In a word that was to become emblematic of this rationale in years to come, promoting greater "transparency" with regard to military affairs in Europe was to be the main purpose of CBMs. Greater transparency, in turn, was expected to reduce the mutual suspicion that secrecy tends to breed and to reflect. In theory, this strategy would lessen the chances that war might come about as a result of misunderstanding or miscalculation.

According to this theory, increasing the transparency or openness of military activities in Europe might lessen fears that a surprise attack could occur or that military exercises could be used successfully for political intimidation. When explained in terms of a hierarchy of arms control objectives, therefore, CBMs could be said to promote the immediate objective of increasing transparency. This increase would then promote higher level arms control objectives, such as reducing miscalculation and misunderstanding, which in turn would support even higher level objectives such as preventing war and preserving peace.[5]

But there were few illusions about the ability of CBMs to promote these higher level arms control objectives any time soon, especially among the superpowers and their allies. The absence of any specific verification provisions for the Helsinki measures, their nonbinding character as voluntary *political*—as opposed to mandatory *legal*—measures, and even their lack of definitional rigor (e.g., the term "major military movement" was left completely undefined) effectively undercut any hopes that the Helsinki CBMs might go beyond the goal of promoting greater military transparency by reducing secrecy.

According to the theory of increasing transparency, the mere fact that the side conducting a potentially threatening activity tells the other side about it tends to reduce anxiety levels. Is this a good thing, or could such measures be used to promote a false sense of confidence? In certain situations, greater apprehension might be warranted. For example, what if the notification of an exercise, even the invitation of observers to attend it, were a clever prelude to a surprise attack? Critics of early CBM theory were quick to raise such questions and to diminish the potential utility of the measures because of negative answers to those questions. The dual effect of CBMs in promoting transparency—that is, they can reduce apprehensiveness but, in the process, can conceivably build false confidence—was a theoretical problem that the first generation of confidence-building measures could not solve.

Second-Generation CBMs

A new generation of CBMs grew out of the attempt to solve this and other problems. Born in the wake of the Soviet invasion of Afghanistan in 1979, as well as Soviet threats to Poland in the early 1980s, the new measures were both an outgrowth of and a reaction to the virtual disappearance of détente in East-West relations. It was one thing to worry about false confidence being generated by CBMs in a period of declining tensions and increasing arms control. It was quite another matter to contemplate this problem as tensions were mounting and CBMs were being used, as they were by the Soviet Union against Poland in 1981, to magnify the signals of political intimidation that were clearly being sent by Soviet military exercises and force deployments.[6]

Furthermore, because of the precipitate decline of détente, the early 1980s were temporarily bereft of traditional arms control efforts. SALT II was suspended, the Strategic Arms Reduction Talks (START) took long to unfold, the Soviets initially refused Intermediate-range Nuclear Forces (INF) negotiations, and things slowed to even less than their customary snail's pace in MBFR. On this barren landscape, two outcroppings appeared that later yielded substantial fruit.

One of these was the effort initiated by U.S. senators Sam Nunn and John Warner to ease tensions in the United States (e.g., in the nuclear freeze movement), as well as in Europe (e.g., in the opposition to NATO's INF deployment decision), over interruption of the superpower dialogue. The two senators proposed that the United States negotiate new crisis management tools with the Soviet Union and that these include, if feasible, nuclear risk reduction centers manned simultaneously and continuously by both sides. These proposals ultimately resulted in new U.S.-Soviet agreements to add a facsimile transmission capability to the hot line (signed in 1984) and to establish nuclear risk reduction centers in Washington and Moscow (signed in 1987), primarily to exchange the information and notifications required under other agreements on arms control or CBMs.[7]

The other effort that grew and developed in the arms control wasteland of the early 1980s was the attempt to negotiate a new and improved set of CBMs for conventional forces in Europe. This effort reached fruition in the Stockholm Document on Confidence- and Security-Building Measures of 1986. The addition of "security" to the title of CBMs in that document, thereby making them "CSBMs," signified that new objectives had been devised for these measures. In the language of the document, which took over six years to negotiate (not only in Stockholm itself but also at the Madrid review meeting of the CSCE, where agreement even to hold the Stockholm talks took three years to reach), the new measures were to be more "militarily significant, binding, and verifiable" than their predecessors. They were to have more politico-military bite, hence a greater security component, as protective compensation for the sharp downturn in East-West relations.

As negotiated in Stockholm, the new CSBMs consisted of the following *mandatory* measures:

- notification forty-two (versus twenty-one) days in advance of major military exercises or concentrations of force (whether movements or maneuvers) involving lower thresholds (e.g., 13,000 troops or 300 tanks versus 25,000 troops);

- notification only at the time of their commencement of certain otherwise notifiable exercises (e.g., alerts);
- exchange of annual calendars by November 15 of all military activities subject to prior notification in the next year;
- invitation of observers to all exercises or concentrations in excess of 17,000 troops (5,000 for amphibious or airborne troops);
- OSI by challenge, subject to a limit of three on any one country's territory per year; and
- constraints on the ability to conduct large-scale exercises (40,000–70,000 troops) that others were not notified of in the preceding one (for 40,000) or two (for 70,000) years.

In contrast to the CBMs discussed above, this package of CSBMs, while still focused on transparency measures for improving information and notification, was more heavily weighted toward access measures (nondiscretionary observation and inspection provisions) than its Helsinki predecessor. It even took a first step in the direction of constraint measures by imposing a variety of longer lead times—forty-two days for major military exercises and one to two years in the case of large-scale exercises—before activities subject to prior notification could occur.

The theory behind these CSBMs was no longer merely that of transparency. Greater openness was still an immediate objective, of course, one that figured prominently in the Stockholm Document's various notification requirements. But the negotiations in Stockholm featured an additional proposal to create a multinational consultative mechanism for the face-to-face exchange of information. One hope for this proposal was that it might evolve into a crisis management center for Europe along the lines that Senators Nunn and Warner were proposing for the United States and the Soviet Union. In the spirit of the times, some suggested that CSBMs themselves might be better understood as tools for the management of crises that otherwise might escalate to nuclear conflict; thus, they too should be considered nuclear risk reduction measures.[8]

In addition to proposals for special consultative mechanisms (which were ultimately unsuccessful at Stockholm) and proposals for notification of specified activities in advance (which were adopted), other requirements were included in the Stockholm Document to ensure that any information provided as a result of increased transparency (for example, through the annual calendar requirement or the lower thresholds) could be verified. Hence, the provisions for mandatory invitation of observers to exercises involving more than 17,000 troops (5,000 in the case of amphibious and airborne troops) and for OSIs by challenge, with no right of refusal. The aim of the new CSBMs was to guarantee that seeing was indeed tantamount to believing. As noted above, this situation had not been the case for CBMs in earlier eras.

The new objective for CSBMs, therefore, included not only prevention of war by misunderstanding or miscalculation (hence the need for greater transparency) but also a reduction in the possibilities for surprise attack and even, if possible, in the ability to use military forces for political intimidation, as the Soviets had in Poland. They key to the success of the new measures lay in their provision of independent means for verification of compliance and intent. A potential attacker could still attempt to mask preparations for war and maintain opportunities for surprise by continuing to comply with the CSBM regime to the last possible moment. The hope was, however, that such continuing compliance with the notification requirements would force a degradation in attack preparations and that, in any event, preparations would be detected through the measures provided for observation and OSI. If an attacker were to refuse to permit observations or inspections in hopes of preserving secrecy, that refusal would send a warning to the defender.

Thus, CSBMs sought to prevent war by increasing the transparency of military activities and by creating a telltale double bind for the potential attacker should increased transparency alone fail to provide the defender with accurate information. The objective was a worthy one and the Stockholm CSBMs came surprisingly close to achieving it. The negotiators' hopes for success hinged largely on the Stockholm Document's verification measure, which for the first time provided for OSIs to be invoked at the discretion of the inspecting side. However, the number of such inspections that the Stockholm Document permits on any given state's territory in any given year—three—is probably too low to guarantee that a potential surprise attacker would ever be faced with a double bind. The number of such inspections may be even too small to prevent misunderstanding or miscalculation, although nothing prevents a state from waiving its rights, upping the quota, and permitting additional inspections on its territory in the interests of clarifying an ambiguous situation and preserving the peace. (In a crisis, this action would itself be a CBM.)

Furthermore, it is not clear that the Stockholm Document's notification thresholds themselves are low enough to complicate a determined attacker's plans for surprise. It is conceivable that such an attacker could artfully make all the preparations necessary within the calendar and notification requirements established, endure several OSIs without detection of the hidden intent, and go on to launch a surprise attack successfully— perhaps more so because of overt, up-to-the-last-minute compliance with the CSBM regime. Such compliance may not enable a potential attacker to mask other indicators of hostile intent, but it might help confuse the defender's attempt to assess the full significance of these other indicators.

Although such a scenario is conceivable, it may be highly unlikely because the risks of random detection are too great. CSBMs measurably improved on CBMs in this regard. Attempts to improve them further—for example, by expanding information exchanges, improving access quotas, lowering thresholds for notifications, and establishing a risk reduction center for Europe—have been on the agenda of successor CSBM negotiations. These have taken place in Vienna since March 1989 in parallel with the successor to the MBFR talks, the negotiations on Conventional Forces in Europe (CFE).

In the end, the Stockholm Document's CSBMs were neither foolproof nor likely to limit the use of force for political intimidation.[9] As permitted by the Stockholm Document, large-scale military exercises conducted as alerts—requiring notification only upon their commencement, not in advance—could still be staged with impunity during a crisis. This activity could tend to exacerbate, rather than dampen, the potential for escalation and intimidation.[10]

Third-Generation CSBMs

In the area of East-West military competition, the world of the late 1980s appeared to be a kinder and gentler place than it had been in any other decade since World War II. Détente-like conditions had returned to the fore, the arms control industry was booming again, and the prospects for peace and prosperity topping everyone's agenda for Europe had never been brighter. In particular, the limits of possible conventional arms control appeared to be significantly expandable, at least for the near term. Soviet President Mikhail Gorbachev's speech to the UN in December 1988 clearly placed conventional arms control high on the list of East-West priorities and helped reduce perceptions of the Soviet Union as a threat. This effect was compounded when the Soviets stood by without interfering as fundamental political changes swept over their former allies in central and eastern Europe.

Into this world, where so many things seemed feasible that had been out of the question before, a new generation of CSBMs appeared ready to debut. These measures promised to set limits or constraints on conventional military forces that were much tighter and more direct than any thus far. Instead of trying to limit military exercises indirectly, as the Stockholm Document did through calendar notification requirements of up to two years in advance, the new measures simply banned the activities outright. If exercises above a certain threshold were a problem, exercises at those levels would be prohibited. If high readiness levels among units were the issue, constraint measures would define and prohibit unacceptable levels. If the problem involved limiting the deployment of particular forces in certain areas—so-called "keep-out" zones—then these forces could be specifically banned from those areas.

Constraints of this type were formally proposed in the context of negotiations on CFE, not in the follow-on CSBM talks that commenced simultaneously in March 1989 in Vienna. To accompany the force reductions that it was advocating in CFE negotiations, NATO put forward a package of proposals that included measures for information exchange, stabilization, and verification. Most of these measures resemble CSBMs in the ways that they were intended to operate. For example, the NATO package included a requirement that all parties be notified forty-two days in advance of call-ups of 40,000 or more reservists within the CFE treaty area; a system of inspections that allowed all parties to the treaty to inspect each other's forces and activities at virtually any time; and a quintessential transparency measure, namely, a call for each side to disclose the exact location of its military units as well as the quantity and types of its treaty-limited equipment.

This same NATO package, however, also included constraint measures of the type described above. The package contained provisions for placing various types of military equipment (e.g., tanks, artillery, armored troop carriers, and bridging equipment) in monitored storage sites and for limiting the amount of such equipment that could be removed from storage at any given time. It also barred signatories of the treaty from conducting military exercises with more than 40,000 troops or 800 main battle tanks more than once every two years. NATO proposed notification of such exercises a year in advance, as well as notification forty-two days in advance of any movement of equipment that exceeded specified amounts (600 tanks, 400 artillery pieces, 1,200 armored troop carriers) or that came out of the storage sites.[11]

NATO's original package of measures to accompany force reductions in CFE, therefore, was robust and comprehensive. The proposal included some of the most demanding information and inspection provisions yet seen in arms control. In addition, it contemplated real and direct limits—that is, constraints—on how the forces that would remain after CFE reductions could be used.

Constraint measures deal more forthrightly and directly with the theoretical problem that CSBMs attempt to solve through the synergistic effect of notification and inspection measures, which, in combination, are intended to confront a potential attacker with the problem of a double bind. Constraints sharpen that bind by establishing prohibitions on military activities that are significant, easier to define, and relatively easy to verify. Any violations of these prohibitions are grounds for serious and immediate concern.

As in the case of CSBMs, robust verification measures, such as the OSI regime that NATO proposed for CFE, add confidence to the value of the information afforded by constraints. In the case of constraints, however, the prohibitions involved are clearer and more direct, with fewer loopholes. CSBM notification requirements provide their own built-in exceptions—for example, alert exercises, even those that exceed the thresholds required for substantial advance notification, can be called on a moment's notice at the discretion of the side conducting the exercises. In theory, constraint measures allow no such exceptions; however, as envisaged in the original NATO proposal, any nation "that believes 'extraordinary events' endanger its 'supreme interests' may withdraw from the proposed conventional arms-control treaty after giving three months' notice."[12]

Pressures of time and the priority accorded to force reductions, however, produced a CFE treaty on November 19, 1990, from which activity-oriented constraint measures were absent. The final agreement, in fact, virtually ignores military activities. It focuses almost entirely on the numerical levels and posttreaty locations of military forces defined in terms of their equipment inventories.

Although they might provide a useful—even necessary—complement to force reductions, there is no reason in theory why constraints or other activity-oriented measures cannot be negotiated independently of future arms reduction agreements. Even in the absence of such agreements, certain types of constraints (e.g., strict limits on the movement of forces outside of their garrisons) might provide a useful substitute for force reductions. With or without reductions, if constraints are combined with effective verification measures, such as the "small army of inspectors" that NATO planned to have visiting Warsaw Pact military units "at short notice, with no right of refusal," they could add significantly to the warning time available in advance of a conflict.[13]

Because they were presented for negotiation in the CFE, the constraint measure and the two notification provisions proposed there were not included in the parallel CSBM talks in Vienna, nor have any comparable measures been adopted in Vienna or in other talks. The CSBM negotiations have focused, for the most part, on revisiting and fleshing out agenda items originally introduced in Stockholm. To this end, they have produced a sweeping information exchange provision, which rivals the CFE treaty's requirements for data; they have established an obligation for consultation and cooperation as regards "unusual and unscheduled" military activities, without defining specific thresholds for such activities; and they have created a mechanism for implementing this obligation—in particular, a Conflict Prevention Center (CPC) in Vienna comprising all thirty-four CSCE participants. In other areas as well, the CSBM negotiations have made improvements on the previously existing Stockholm measures.[14] Some constraints on military activities, for example, have been agreed upon, and the notification and constraint provisions adopted in Vienna in early 1992 are more stringent than those originally developed at Stockholm.

Comparing Europe and the Middle East

While the United States and European nations have evolved the series of formal arms control and CBMs described above, the countries of the Middle East, despite their many unresolved conflicts, have produced examples of practical restraint—including the highly sophisticated demilitarization agreements between Israel and Syria regarding the Golan Heights and between Israel and Egypt regarding the Sinai. Of particular relevance is the Egyptian-Israeli peace treaty that was finally consummated in April 1982. The treaty had its origin in agreements negotiated among the United States, Israel, and Egypt between 1974 and 1979 and during Egyptian President Anwar Sadat's historic trip to Jerusalem in 1977. One reason this treaty has survived is because it is buttressed by complex arms control agreements that limit military activity in the Sinai Peninsula and along the Egyptian-Israeli border and that include the currently deployed Multinational Force and Observers (MFO).[15]

At both the political and strategic level, however, the differences between Europe and the Middle East are very wide. Most important, neither NATO nor the Warsaw Pact seriously considered using military force against each other, given the presence of large numbers of nuclear weapons in the European theater and the explicit linkage between the use of conventional arms and the use of nuclear weapons. A NATO-Warsaw Pact war was widely perceived to be a remote possibility, primarily because no one could see how either side could win. In contrast, Middle Eastern countries have amply demonstrated their belief that force, as a last resort, is a necessary instrument of national policy. Furthermore, victory in war has brought rewards, at least in the short run, to the winning side. Israel, for instance, has been able to buy itself many years of security by defeating the Arabs in a number of wars. However, the Arabs have not been deterred from fighting Israel. Instead, they considered the 1973 war against Israel necessary to redeem their pride, improve their bargaining position with outside powers, and persuade Israel to relinquish territories captured in the 1967 war. Syria and Iraq have used force on many occasions against other neighbors, and the wars in North Africa indicate that military conflict remains an acceptable method of coercive diplomacy elsewhere in the region.

Further differences reveal the chasm separating the European experience from that of the Middle East. As discussed earlier, initial CBSMs and arms control agreements were reached in Europe before the Gorbachev era at the height of the Cold War. There were good reasons why these agreements were possible. First, a balance of power already existed. Two major offsetting alliances, NATO and the Warsaw Pact, backed by the nuclear weapons of the superpowers, ensured that no small country or group of countries within the European arena could fundamentally upset this balance. In addition, although border disputes sometimes arose between European powers, it was generally agreed that force should not be used to resolve them. Indeed, since 1975 there has been formal agreement in Europe, enshrined in the Helsinki Final Act of that year and the Charter of Paris in 1990, that war is an illegitimate instrument of policy when it comes to changing borders.

Even at the height of the Cold War, U.S., Soviet, western, and most eastern European diplomats were meeting regularly. The European powers, the former Soviet Union, and the United States have cooperated on many issues since World War II.

Although these relations did not prevent the Cold War, at no point were relations so bad that all communication ceased. Eventually, the NATO and Warsaw Pact countries came to appreciate that arms limitations and troop reductions would translate directly into enhanced security for all parties. This appreciation was the commonality that drove the process forward, at least at the planning level, before political decisions were taken to implement concrete measures.

Recent progress on European arms control can be attributed to the strength of the NATO alliance, to Gorbachev's reform policies, and to the subsequent relaxation of East-West tensions. Political will on both sides pushed for reductions. There was a mutual desire for domestic retrenchment. There were no imminent security threats to either alliance or to any individual member of either alliance. Sources of tension had begun to break down, particularly as glasnost and perestroika removed many of the fears and misperceptions on both sides. Finally, the ideological aspects of the Cold War were no longer seen as a zero-sum struggle between the two parties.

It is difficult to find counterparts to these trends in the Middle East despite breakthroughs in face-to-face negotiations. Most countries in the region face multiple threats from their neighbors. Although some major conflicts (Arab-Israeli, Iran-Iraq) have widespread regional significance, other potential bilateral conflicts are also intense and dangerous. Hence, no single military standoff exists between two groups such as NATO and the Warsaw Pact.

By reducing the Iraqi military threat, the Persian Gulf War altered the regional power structure, giving Israel more prominence as the dominant regional hegemon. In particular, Israel's nuclear capability is seen by the Arab states as unilaterally skewing the balance of power and demonstrating asymmetries in military capabilities. Israel regards the balance as equally distorted, with the Arabs having the advantages of geography, demography, and wealth. In sum, there is no basic parity in

force levels or in types of weaponry and the region is characterized by massive asymmetries in force structure, including
the quality and quantity of arms.

In marked contrast to Europe, secure and accepted legal
boundaries remain a key source of antagonism in the Middle
East. The territorial issues between Israel and all its neighbors,
except Egypt, remain unresolved. There are territorial disputes
between Syria and Lebanon, with Syria claiming it has rights
over all of Lebanon. The Iran-Iraq War began as a battle over
the delineation of the boundaries along the Shatt al-Arab wa-
terway. Unlike Europe, there are no accepted geographic parameters of the region for arms control agreements or political
dialogue to take as points of departure. To define what is meant
by the Middle East is complicated, particularly as the dynamics
of the region change. It will become even more difficult in the
future as new Muslim states emerge in the wake of the Soviet
Union's disintegration.

The absence of diplomatic relations between Israel and all the
Arab nations except Egypt is also a major stumbling block to
the peace process. This problem directly relates to the question
of Palestinian rights. Although an Arab-Israeli political dialogue has begun, until the issues of Israel's borders, its right to
exist, and the political rights of the Palestinians are resolved, it
is difficult to envisage significant arms control initiatives taking
place.

In the Middle East, there is little recognition at this time that
arms control, or arms reductions, will serve national or mutual
interests. To approximate the European model, there must be a
shared desire to promote stability and improve relations. There
must also be an absence of imminent security threats. None of
these conditions currently pertains in the Middle East, and none
is likely to emerge in the absence of some breakthrough on one
or more diplomatic fronts. Nevertheless, precursor CSBMs are
not only possible but might even be embraced by the region.

Some of the reasons for this conclusion are explained in the following sections.

The Changing Climate for CSBMs

The Madrid and Washington meetings among Israel, Jordan, Lebanon, Syria, and the Palestinians provided the first openings in a peace process that will likely be protracted and impassioned. Serious arms control initiatives will likely be too sensitive to consider in the early rounds of negotiations, which will probably focus on procedural issues and general statements of principle. For this reason, precursor CBMs in the security arena—CBMs designed to strengthen the resolve of the parties to stay with the negotiations—could be helpful. More bluntly stated, precursor CBMs may be essential to the process, given the proclivity of countries in the region to continue antagonizing each other and creating mistrust rather than confidence. (Included in this category would be continued violence by Arab groups against Israel and Israeli settlement activity in the occupied territories.) Small incremental steps are needed at this time rather than grandiose schemes for Arab-Israeli arms control. These steps must be linked to progress in peace negotiations.

After all, arms control covers a wide variety of initiatives—unilateral, bilateral, and multilateral—and can cover the gamut from informal CBMs, such as "red lines" that establish military ground rules between adversaries, to formal multilateral treaties that eliminate entire classes of armaments, such as nuclear and chemical weapons. The peace process refers to a complicated series of negotiations between adversaries that passes through at least three distinct but integrally linked stages: prenegotiations, negotiations, and postnegotiations. At each stage, different agreements are necessary to move the process forward and different arms control initiatives are appropriate.

At present, there are no serious negotiations on the peace process but because arms control, including confidence building, is already on the peace agenda, the negotiating parties are taking their first steps toward understanding what these concepts mean and how to address them in both bilateral and multilateral meetings. Because major arms control initiatives are premature, it makes sense to pursue confidence-building agendas prior to Arab-Israeli reconciliation and to accept that substantive progress on more far-reaching arms control must wait (as it had to wait in Europe) until the political environment has improved. The overall Arab-Israeli conflict is still in the prenegotiation phase; that is, all parties have shown some interest in a peace settlement but disagree on how to proceed. Limited CBMs already exist and new ones might contribute to an atmosphere more conducive to negotiations.

Indeed, there have been indications, discernible before the Persian Gulf War, that both Egypt and Israel regard further arms control proposals as a legitimate issue for discussion. There are political and military reasons for this new attitude. Given the nature of the arms race, the concern is that if military procurement trends continue, the dangers of war and the costs of deterrence will grow. Also, because of the dramatic developments in East-West dialogue on conflict resolution, pressures are building on regional leaders to take similar steps. Otherwise, the major arms-supplier countries, in their new spirit of cooperation to resolve regional conflicts, may initiate Middle East arms control regimes that the regional powers find intrusive. The local parties may conclude that because the chance of any serious progress on regional arms control is remote, they have little to lose by appearing conciliatory and willing to discuss the highly complex issues in their security relationships.

Perhaps most important, although few political leaders in the region believe that a full-scale, premeditated Arab-Israeli war is imminent, most agree that the danger of a major crisis, or war by miscalculation, is cause for concern. Thus, while the wisdom of arms control restraints may be questioned, there is consensus on the need for measures to prevent wars by miscalculation and to limit the consequences should such wars occur.[16]

Reducing the Risks of War by Miscalculation

Israel and those Arab neighbors with whom it is still technically at war must find ways to avoid miscalculations about one another's military intentions. Two incidents over the past few years could have led to inadvertent war: the first, between Israel and Syria; the second, between Israel and Iraq.

In April 1986 Nizar Hindawi, a Syrian terrorist originally from Jordan, attempted to smuggle explosives onto an El Al flight leaving London's Heathrow Airport bound for Israel. The explosives were detected and removed, and Hindawi, after approaching the Syrian embassy in London for help, turned himself in to the British police.[17] If the El Al plane had been destroyed and its more than 200 passengers killed, Israel would almost certainly have taken harsh military measures against Syria that could have led to all-out war. If one assumes that Syrian President Assad did not want a war and was unaware of the Hindawi plot, then one way to avoid future incidents would be some form of tacit Israeli-Syrian cooperation to strengthen intelligence gathering on terrorist operations that could damage both countries.

The second event concerned an explosion that took place in Iraq in September 1989, when it was reported that a missile production facility outside Baghdad had blown up.[18] On March 15, 1990, a journalist working for the London Observer who had been caught illegally investigating the site of the explosion was hanged in Baghdad. At that time, it was feared that Saddam Hussein might attribute another accident in an Iraqi munitions plant to Israel. Under certain circumstances, this occurrence could have caused Hussein to attack Israel in the expectation that if he did not, he would lose all his forces if Israel attacked Iraq. Mechanisms to convey information to each side about such a crisis might dispel fears of a surprise or preemptive attack. Before the Persian Gulf Crisis there was some talk of exploring ways to establish an Israel-Iraq hot line, possibly using the good offices of Egypt; there is reason to believe that such efforts may now fall on receptive ears among a number of the countries in the region.

Transparency

All sides in the Arab-Israeli conflict are deeply suspicious of each other's military capabilities and intentions. This atmosphere suggests that greater transparency could be helpful and should be seriously explored. One complicating factor concerns Israel's nuclear weapons program. The post–Persian Gulf War arms control debate has focused increased attention on Israel's nuclear arsenal and the general issue of regional nuclear proliferation. President Bush's May 1991 initiative offered a cautious but sensible approach for dealing with these issues. By calling for a freeze on further nuclear proliferation in the region rather than outright abolition, the initiative attempted to deal with the threat that the spread of nuclear weapons poses, while respecting Israel's security requirements. It is plausible that Israel would agree to halt further production of nuclear weapons, provided it was convinced that the Arab states would not acquire the same weapons. In any case, by raising these issues, the Bush administration has potentially laid the groundwork for far greater transparency about Middle East security concerns.[19]

Experience with Red Lines

"Red lines" refer to informal agreements between adversaries concerning limits on the deployment and use of armed forces in given geographic regions. Red lines have been integral to both formal and informal force separation agreements in the

Arab-Israeli conflict. They have been used in two ways. First, in the literal sense, red lines can refer to geographic lines or boundaries agreed upon by the parties and established as markers beyond which one or both sides will not deploy forces. Second, in a conceptual sense red lines refer to conditions that prohibit certain actions. These, like the geographic lines, can be mutually agreed upon or simply laid out by one party.

In April 1976, Syria and Israel reached a secret agreement through U.S. mediation to minimize their chances of confrontation in Lebanon. Syria agreed to Israeli red line conditions allowing Syrian military intervention in Lebanon provided it was restricted to ground forces and that these forces did not move south of a line between the Zaharani estuary of the Mediterranean and the village of Mashki in the Bekka Valley. As part of this agreement, Syria was to respect Israel's legitimate security concerns in southern Lebanon and to avoid air attacks against Christian targets.[20]

Israel and Jordan also have an informal red line agreement. Because historic attack routes suggest an invading Arab army would come from the east through Jordan, Israeli military strategists have consistently viewed Jordan's eastern and northern borders as red lines. If Iraqi or Syrian forces entered Jordan in significant numbers, Israeli forces would automatically respond. Understandings between Jordan and Israel on this condition have benefited both countries. For Israel, such a policy reinforces its deterrence posture. For Jordan, this form of agreement bolsters national sovereignty and protects against Syrian and Iraqi intervention. Israel and Jordan also have informal understandings concerning their shared border along the Jordan valley. These understandings have dealt mostly with attempts to combat terrorist infiltration into Israel, thereby reducing the potential for political tension between Amman and Jerusalem.

An additional example of successful deployment limitations sprang from Israeli concerns about Saudi air force deployments.

Strong Israeli opposition to the sale of U.S. F-15s to Saudi Arabia in 1978 led to a U.S.-Saudi understanding on the deployment of the planes in Saudi Arabia. Sixty-two aircraft were eventually sold, but the aircraft were not to be stationed near the Israeli border. Israel was primarily concerned about the construction of an air base at Tabuk in northwest Saudi Arabia. Under pressure from Israel, the United States successfully insisted at that time that none of the new planes be stationed at Tabuk.[21]

It is possible to envisage further red lines between Israel and its neighbors, absent a breakthrough on the peace front. One possibility would be for additional Israeli-Syrian under-standings on the use of force in Lebanon now that the Lebanese army is reestablishing control over parts of southern Lebanon and the power of the Iranian-backed Hezbullah groups has waned.

Weapons-Testing Limitation Possibilities

Similarly, agreements to limit or ban testing of certain weapons systems might also help build confidence. For example, an agreement by Israel not to conduct flight tests of ballistic missiles or not to test a nuclear device would be a significant gesture to its adversaries. If this agreement were paralleled by an Arab agreement not to test ballistic missiles, it would be a useful, reciprocal CBM. Combined with external restraints on the supply of missiles to the region, such a measure could significantly reduce the potential for offensive missile attacks. A ban on testing nuclear weapons could be the first step toward achieving a nuclear-free zone in the Middle East.

Potential CSBMs

At present, the prospects for negotiating formal CSBMs between the adversaries in the Arab-Israeli conflict are not good. This situation should not detract from efforts to establish an

Arab-Israeli dialogue on such measures within the context of the official negotiations. CSBMs, however, are more likely to succeed within less formal settings, where the role of private organizations in establishing the ground rules for CSBMs could be important. The first efforts must be low key and are probably best focused on understanding the threat perceptions of the regional players.

Better understanding of each other's security fears does not of itself ensure an improved political climate. However, if groups of specialists from the region meet and talk about security over a period of months or even years, they may come to trust each other more and may then be prompted to consider more seriously proposals of the kind that have proven successful in Europe. This human dimension of the process cannot be stressed too highly. Even at the height of the Cold War, Soviet diplomats met formally with their western counterparts and Soviet scientists had numerous exchanges with western colleagues in fora such as the Pugwash Meetings and the Dartmouth Group.

By the end of 1991, some tiny chinks in the Middle East official and unofficial walls of suspicion could be detected. Meetings among Syrian, Israeli, Lebanese, Jordanian, and Palestinian officials were underway, albeit without much warmth. It is still difficult for Israeli private citizens to meet informally with their counterparts from Syria and Jordan, and, certainly, it remains impossible for any Israeli to meet Arabs in any Middle East country except Egypt and possibly Morocco. When on rare occasions specialists from most of the region can be brought together, it is clear that there is a marked absence of understanding of the complexities and nuances of the arms control experience.

In sum, there is a major educational job to be done, which involves recruiting and helping influence a new generation of regional officials and specialists who must sort out security problems more complex than those found in Europe. In itself, such an educational process would serve as a significant precursor CBM. Among the issues that should be discussed is a menu of measures that could eventually become part of the architecture of a Middle East settlement, including a variety of CSBMs that were earlier described and analyzed in the European context:

- Information measures, which include information exchange requirements of the kind agreed upon most recently in Vienna. To the extent that the measures include useful details about planned activities, the requirements to notify others of planned military activities (which date back to the Helsinki Final Act and the first generation CBMs) also constitute a form of information exchange.
- Communication measures, which are represented by the U.S.-Soviet hot line and its various offshoots and upgrades, as well as by consultative arrangements of the kind embodied in the Conflict Prevention Center (CPC), recently agreed upon in Vienna.
- Access measures, which have included provisions for observers at notified military activities ever since the Helsinki Final Act. Such provisions were progressively improved as a result of the subsequent negotiations in Stockholm and Vienna. This category also includes on-site inspection measures of the kind first agreed upon in Stockholm.
- Notification measures, which essentially permit military activities to occur but attach certain conditions to them. Such measures not only require participants to inform each other (preferably far in advance) that they are or will be engaging in significant military activities, but also implicitly enjoin participants to refrain from undertaking certain activities that they have not notified others of in advance. Stockholm's requirements for forty-two-day advance notification of field exercises fall

into this category, as do the Vienna CFE negotiation's abortive proposal to treat the call-up reservists in the same fashion.

- Constraint measures, which attempt to prohibit specified activities. In contrast to notification measures, which are essentially permissive of military activities (provided the parties are indeed notified), constraints seek to discourage certain activities, if not ban them outright. The Stockholm Document's fledgling constraint measure for large-scale military exercises moved in this direction. More ambitious constraints might seek to prohibit specified exercises without exception.

If the history of these different measures in Europe is any guide, it suggests that only information, communication, and access measures, as well as some shorter-term notification measures, seem likely candidates for adoption in the Middle East in the near future. This presumes, of course, that it eventually becomes possible to venture beyond precursor CSBMs in the region. Tougher notification and constraint measures have thus far proven impossible to negotiate in Europe. Hence, it may be unrealistic to assume that similar or more ambitious measures are likely to be adopted elsewhere.

It is tempting to conclude that nothing in the way of confidence building or arms control as developed in Europe is possible in the Middle East. Parties that, in some cases, do not even recognize each other's existence are going to have serious trouble building confidence among themselves. Over time and with the experience gained from implementing a modest set of precursor measures, however, it may be possible to expand the scope of measures that can be negotiated. Hopes and expectations for CSBMs applied to regions beyond Europe, however, will probably have to remain limited for some time to come. But within the limits—which initially seemed too restrictive and unpromising in Europe as well—useful initiatives can be launched and new beginnings cultivated.

Despite the political difficulties inherent in the Middle East, it is not only possible but also practical to conceive of a regime of CSBMs operating in that troubled region. The case of UN forces having managed a regime of on-site challenge inspections of both Israeli and Syrian forces in the Golan Heights since 1974, as noted above, clearly shows that much can be done, even between countries that are still at war and do not recognize each other. One can envisage, for example, specified information on force structures and notification of certain impending military activities being provided to a third party (e.g., the UN), which then shares that information with other participants in the regime. One can even imagine the third party furnishing observers or inspectors to monitor the activities and provide reports that are shared among all participants. One can also imagine the third party serving not only as a data collector and disseminator but also as a mediator through which some parties communicate—indirectly—with each other.

Although a direct approach would be preferable, it does not seem to be a real option now for the Middle East as a whole. In cases where direct approaches cannot be pursued (e.g., between Israel and most Arab states), the indirect approach is preferable to no approach at all. At a minimum, even under an indirect or third-party approach, military information would start to be shared more readily than it is at present. Transparency would increase to some extent and predictable patterns of military activity stand a chance of being established. In peacetime such developments can help prevent a crisis by reducing the chances that military activities will occur unexpectedly and precipitate a crisis. In a crisis, even an indirect approach that is already in place and continues to operate can provide a channel for communication and escalation control that would not otherwise exist.

An outside party such as the United Nations, or the United States, which might serve as the intermediary for CBM-type measures in the Middle East, would have to play a highly active role in the process of negotiating and implementing such measures. This third party may have to recommend an initial set of measures for adoption and then negotiate that set, individually, with each of the other parties. That challenge is difficult, but it could be eased somewhat by recommending a set of measures—for example, an adaptation of the Helsinki and Stockholm CSBMs or of the U.S.-Soviet agreements on incidents at sea or dangerous military activities—that already have a certain standing and track record within the international community.

A former U.S. ambassador to the Stockholm talks, James E. Goodby, suggests that a "maximum effort" package of "transparency" measures—information, communication, access, and notification measures that have either been adopted or seriously considered in Europe—might ultimately be applied in the Middle East. Goodby's ten-point plan includes the following:

- Establishment of a CPC, of the kind recently created in Europe, for the Middle East, or a third-party mechanism performing the same functions through the UN;
- Annual exchanges of data on types, quantities, and deployments of major military equipment through the CPC or third parties;
- A specified number of visits each year to the territories of each of the parties involved to confirm the accuracy of the data exchanged;
- Notification forty-five days in advance through the CPC or third parties of any out-of-garrison movements, maneuvers, or concentrations of military forces above agreed-on thresholds;
- Observation by either CPC or third-party representatives of out-of-garrison military activities that are subject to notification, including short-notice alert and mobilization exercises lasting more than twenty-four hours;

- A specified number of on-site inspections of each participant's territory each year by CPC or third-party representatives;
- An explanation by a participant of any unusual military activities it is undertaking; in lieu of an adequate explanation, inspection of such activities by the CPC, third parties, or their national technical means of verification;
- An "open skies" aerial monitoring system operated by the CPC or third parties;
- A hot line for rapid communications among participants, including, if necessary, a CPC or third parties;
- Annual meetings of participants' military chiefs of staff with the CPC or with third parties to review past implementation, future military activities, and planned acquisition and deployment of major weapons systems.[22]

Although this entire list currently has little hope for adoption, once a first set of measures has been agreed on—for example, hot lines and aerial monitoring by third parties as precursor CSBMs—and implemented, it may be possible for a third party such as the UN to coax Middle East participants farther down the path traveled earlier (and more directly) by their European and U.S. counterparts. Both the multilateral European and the bilateral U.S.-Soviet cases suggest that it should be possible to negotiate more of the CSBMs on Goodby's list once a reasonably successful track record has been established with an initial set of measures.

Thomas J. Hirschfeld, a former MBFR negotiator, however, has recommended an approach to arms control in the Middle East that differs significantly from the one advanced here. Hirschfeld argues that even if undertakings to negotiate European-style CSBMs could somehow be arranged in the Middle East through interested third parties, differences in circumstances between Arabs and Israelis "would render most of these measures difficult to implement, or useless." He suggests, for example, that requirements to have movements of forces out of garrison prenotified and observed would probably not interest Arab countries, because many "potential Arab force concentrations, even concentrations near Israel, have purposes not directly or immediately related to attacking or confronting Israel. ... And Israel, which relies on prompt mobilization in response to warning, could hardly welcome the dilemma of choosing between violating a hypothetical agreement (say, with Egypt) to preannounce all large call-ups, or mobilizing rapidly to face threats from Syria."[23]

Instead of arms control analogues drawn directly from the European experience, Hirschfeld proposes six measures that he believes might hold more promise for the Middle East. These measures seem to derive more from U.S.-Soviet or Israeli-Egyptian negotiating experiences than from that of Europe. The measures include the following:

- Zones of caution in frontier areas, noninterference with communications, and military consultations akin to the U.S.-Soviet dangerous military activities agreement noted earlier;
- Prohibition of concealment to overhead observation (for missile forces);
- Advance notification of missile firing tests;
- Open skies overhead observation—if possible, through commercially available satellites; if necessary, through third parties;
- Prearranged channels for continued communication through third parties in the event of a crisis or hostilities;
- Prearranged sites, predesignated third-party mediators, and prearranged communication channels to control escalation (e.g., further missile launches) and facilitate termination of a conflict.[24]

Hirschfeld's proposals are cautious and sensible, particularly to the extent that they draw on those U.S.-Soviet arms control experiences that can supply useful precedents for the Middle

East. Although his dismissal of "most of the Europe-centered East-West experience with confidence-building measures" as "inapplicable for the moment" to the Middle East is fair,[25] both Goodby's ten-point plan and this chapter suggest that one should not underestimate the spillover effect of transparency measures drawn from the European experience. If that experience is any indication, "a day-to-day process of security cooperation, including routine exchanges of critical security information and regular contact among military observers on all sides" can have profound effects.[26]

At face value, such measures may seem problematical and not all that worthwhile, as Hirschfeld contends, but over time they can help alleviate the fears and tensions that breed conflict. Although one cannot argue that these measures produced the sweeping political changes that swept over Europe in the late 1980s, CSBMs did help create a kind of infrastructure that increased military transparency in Europe. One can argue that this infrastructure helped make it possible to accelerate the effect of political changes in the military sphere (with monumental arms control treaties such as INF and CFE, for example) once the changes had begun.

Once again, however, the lessons learned from the historical cases explored here suggest that the going will be slow—even slower, one would think, if an indirect, third-party approach is pursued in the Middle East. Nevertheless, the lessons learned from Europe also suggest that possibilities for progress will be continually available, even in times of political setback and crisis. Dramatic breakthroughs achieved primarily through CSBMs or other arms control agreements seem highly unlikely in the Middle East. Such developments appear destined to await more fundamental changes in political relationships between and among opposing parties. In the meantime, CSBM arms control efforts of the kind explored here can help establish useful, if not necessarily decisive, preconditions for political change. They can also help speed the process on its way if and when the change occurs.

3. The Role of Aerial Inspections in Confidence Building and Peacemaking

Michael Krepon and Peter D. Constable

Confidence-building measures (CBMs) have been defined as "arrangements designed to enhance ... assurance of mind and belief in the trustworthiness of states and the facts they create."[1] CBMs, by definition, must promote confidence on both sides of any dispute. Nonsymmetrical or unilateral measures not acceptable to the other side tend to increase rather than decrease tensions.[2]

If states in the Middle East wish to create facts associated with trustworthiness and peacemaking, a wide range of CBMs might be employed to lessen tensions, quiet borders, or introduce a measured degree of transparency that does not impinge on the security of any participating state. A significant number of these measures—some publicly acknowledged, some not—have already been employed in various parts of the Middle East to mitigate the Arab-Israeli dispute and tensions in other parts of the region as well.

Aerial inspections are a unique type of CBM. In theory, aerial inspections can have broad applicability as a CBM. They can be

---

The authors wish to thank William Durch, Alan Platt, and Amy Smithson for their helpful comments on this essay.

used to ease tension along borders, provide an early warning of troubling activities, or confirm data exchanges about the disposition of military forces and the conduct of military exercises. Aerial inspections can also be used to monitor multilateral agreements barring or limiting certain types of weapons. Most important, these inspections can be used to verify formal troop disengagement agreements, thin-out zones, and peace treaties between states.

The Open Skies Treaty, signed in March 1992, provides the most well-developed model of cooperative aerial inspections. More limited forms of cooperative aerial inspections have been carried out quietly and successfully for over three decades.[3] Because the East-West Open Skies Treaty calls for the use of highly capable sensors and far-ranging overflights by foreign nationals, it has logically followed more limited CBMs. Only after a long list of CBMs had been agreed to in bilateral and multilateral accords, ranging from the establishment of communication links to the provision of observers and inspectors at military exercises, did negotiators turn in earnest to the open skies concept at the Conference on Security and Cooperation in Europe (CSCE).

This progression is understandable given deeply rooted concerns about the intelligence-gathering potential of surveillance aircraft and the sensors they carry. The reach of aerial inspections is potentially far greater than that of ground inspections. Aircraft that provide transparency can also provide targeting information, and states that have sophisticated sensors and processing equipment can easily secure advantages in times of war or peace over states with lesser capabilities. When sophisticated and extensive offensive capabilities exist at close proximity in regions of tension, as was the case in central Europe and continues to be the case in the Middle East and on the Korean peninsula, too much transparency has the potential to do more harm than good.

The European progression on CBMs, however, need not be an appropriate model for the Middle East. More limited forms of cooperative aerial inspections may precede data exchanges, formal crisis communication links, and on-site inspections (OSIs), depending on the unique conditions within a troubled region. This situation has, in fact, been the case in the Middle East, where tension levels are appreciably higher than in Europe, where all but one Arab state do not maintain official diplomatic relations with Israel, and where brief but costly and dangerous wars occur on the average of one per decade. Nevertheless, in this violence-racked region, where formal peace treaties are rare and where many CBMs appear to be unacceptable, several countries have accepted and lived with carefully circumscribed aerial inspections for a decade and a half.

The most public of these arrangements have been carried out by the UN peacekeeping operations in Lebanon and along the Iran-Iraq border, and by peacekeepers in the Sinai implementing formal arrangements enshrined in disengagement agreements and the Egyptian-Israeli peace treaty. As discussed below, third-party aerial inspections have also been carried out by the United States to ease tensions over sensitive border areas in the region, but the operation of these arrangements has not been widely publicized.[4]

The existence of cooperative aerial inspections in a tension-filled region such as the Middle East appears to present many theoretical contradictions, yet these operations have produced a quietly successful track record. This record suggests that cooperative aerial inspections might play an expanded role in future attempts to negotiate solutions to a number of territorial and border disputes between some of the Arab states and Israel, particularly as they might help in enhancing border security, observing areas where levels of military personnel and equipment have been limited, and monitoring exclusion or demilitarized zones.

Existing Practices

Three general types of agreed aerial inspections are now carried out on a regular basis in the Middle East. First, arrangements are in place—either formally agreed on or tacitly accepted between former combatants—to allow each side's specially equipped aircraft to fly alongside, but not over, border areas that have been the scene of considerable bloodshed.[5] These national flights on one's own side of the border use sophisticated photographic equipment, some with considerable range. Less sophisticated sensors, which are available commercially from a number of sources including the United States, the former Soviet Union, France, Germany, and perhaps others, presumably are also employed in the region.

These flights can provide a degree of confidence building by demonstrating the absence of attack preparations. Used this way, they clearly help build more confidence than no flights at all. Just as the noninterference provision in the first U.S.-Soviet Strategic Arms Limitation Treaty eventually led to intrusive verification measures, tacitly or formally approved reconnaissance operations in the Middle East may be considered precursor CBMs if they help produce political conditions leading to more substantive measures. The value of these national reconnaissance missions is limited, however, by terrain features, weather, and the lack of OSIs to confirm that no significant concealment of forces is underway.

In effect, these compacts not to interfere with national technical means (NTM) are a regional analogue to similar provisions formally negotiated in agreements to limit U.S. and Soviet strategic offensive and defensive arms. At least one state in the region—Israel—appears intent on having an outer space–based NTM. Given the expense and sporadic coverage of such a limited photo-reconnaissance satellite network, however, all states in the region will surely continue to rely heavily on aerial reconnaissance operations for myriad reasons, including, perhaps, greater confidence building and peacemaking.

The second form of agreed aerial inspections has been carried out by multinational forces under the auspices of the UN or, in the case of the Sinai and a slim strip of Israeli territory adjacent to it, by the Multinational Force and Observers (MFO), with important support and assistance from the United States. The relatively unsophisticated aircraft used for these overflights are based in the region and do not carry sensors.[6]

In the case of the work of the MFO, aerial inspections complement regular OSIs, thus providing a large measure of assurance to the other side that no unauthorized buildups are underway. The combination has demonstrated its worth in reinforcing the security provisions of the Egyptian-Israeli peace treaty. Regardless of how much Israelis may lament the so-called "cold peace" with Egypt, they also understand and value the assurances gained from aerial inspections and OSIs, which make unlikely a repeat of the 1973 Yom Kippur surprise from the west.

Third, Israel, Egypt, and Syria have agreed to limited third-party overflights originating from outside the region along sensitive border areas.[7] For both the Sinai and Golan Heights, regular aerial photography of demilitarized and limited-armament zones has been conducted since 1974 by the United States under UN auspices and made available to the appropriate parties in Egypt, Israel, and Syria. This routine is in addition to the aerial surveillance conducted by national forces, on their respective sides of the UN zones that were provided for in the 1974 Golan Agreement and the successive agreements on the Sinai. The UN's aerial photographic coverage of the Sinai was extended in 1975, as were the Israeli and Egyptian aerial surveillance limits, to cover the larger demilitarized and limited-armament areas specified in the Sinai II disengagement agreement. Third-party coverage was extended again both after signature of the 1979 Egyptian-Israeli peace treaty and following Israel's final withdrawal from the Sinai.

The existence of this coverage has been welcomed and never challenged by the governments of the three countries in question. It may well have contributed significantly, along with other CBMs and verification techniques, to the virtual absence of accusations of threatening military activity by Israel, Egypt, or Syria over the Sinai and Golan Heights since 1974. This situation stands in contrast to the sharp accusations exchanged, the high degree of tension, and the periodic clashes in these areas between 1967 and 1973, including the 1968–70 War of Attrition.

For such aerial operations to succeed, there must be considerable confidence that the third party will conduct overflights with impartiality and in strict accordance in an agreed framework. Such arrangements also imply that the third party will be trusted to interpret accurately the photographic results and, most important, to use its influence with the other parties to deal with any untoward, unauthorized, or otherwise dangerous developments captured in the photography. As the sparseness of the reportable information on these overflights suggests, discretion is often crucial to their success.

Any expanded use of cooperative aerial inspections in the region presumes commitments on the part of political leaders to move toward a reduced level of tension. Aerial inspections cannot possibly substitute for such political commitments. If, however, political leaders are willing to extend themselves in this way, aerial inspections can provide multiple dividends. They can, for example, allow states in the region a cooling-off period in which other diplomatic efforts may be undertaken to alleviate security concerns. Just as states may engage in prenegotiations prior to formal talks on security issues, tacit or formal agreements that acknowledge stabilizing activities already underway—such as aerial reconnaissance operations within one's boundaries—may serve as valuable precursors to more substantive measures.

Such measures might include the use of cooperative aerial inspections to provide additional indications and warnings of troubling developments in the field. In a narrow range of cases, aerial inspections could help deter violations of agreements already reached or, at the least, raise the cost and increase the difficulty of militarily significant violations. Aerial inspections can help reinforce OSIs, orienting inspectors for site visits, allowing them to make the most efficient use of their time on the ground, and providing backup when they get into difficult situations. Ultimately, aerial inspections can play a critical role in monitoring peace treaties between former combatants in the region, as they now do in reinforcing the peace between Egypt and Israel.

If successfully carried out, aerial inspections can provide reassurance, reinforcement, and added effectiveness for peacekeeping forces. To help shed light on how such inspections might be optimally carried out in the Middle East in the future, several conditions that bear on successful aerial inspections will first be reviewed. Operational considerations will then be addressed, and safeguards will be discussed that might alleviate concerns over military targeting and intelligence gathering and, at the same time, accentuate the confidence building nature of aerial inspections. In conclusion, several new and expanded areas for aerial inspections that might further confidence-building and peace efforts in the Middle East will be discussed.

Conditions for Successful Aerial Inspections

There is a marked, and not surprising, correlation between the conditions for successful peacekeeping operations and the conditions for successful aerial inspections in the Middle East.[8] Of the various factors bearing on successful aerial inspections, five stand out. Above all, there must be the political consent of those states whose territory is to be overflown. Second, participating states must have positive control over ground and air forces that could interfere with aerial inspections with tragic consequences. Third, aerial inspections are best carried out under a clear mandate with precise guidelines approved by all participating states. Fourth, the topography of the region to be overflown must be amenable to aerial inspections. Finally, financing must be adequate or donations in kind must be provided for aerial inspections to get off the ground. An additional consideration for the Middle East, although not necessarily a requirement, is discretion. Aerial inspections are by definition intrusive and always raise the specter of "spy missions." To the extent that these factors can be negotiated and implemented in ways sensitive to the often paranoid environment of the Middle East, the chances for success are enhanced.

The first condition listed above provides the basis for all that follow: Cooperative aerial inspections obviously require the political consent of national leaders and their military organizations.[9] Political consent need not imply the expectation that a peace treaty ultimately will result from overflights; instead, political leaders may simply wish to promote a cooling-off period in which the central issues under dispute remain unresolved. Between these two poles, considerable room exists for diplomatic maneuver if national leaders are willing to expend the political capital required to reduce tensions.

Even in the absence of peacemaking efforts, experience in the Middle East suggests that aerial inspections can play a critical role in sustaining a cooling-off period between nations that maintain a formal state of belligerency. It is at least arguable that there would have been no disengagement agreements between Egypt and Israel or between Israel and Syria in the 1970s if the parties had not been able to agree on provisions for third-party aerial inspections.

Properly configured aerial inspections can be helpful simply in preventing conflicts that arise from inadvertent actions or accidents. A formal state of belligerency that does not result in actual combat provides time in which creative diplomacy can be carried out and in which new political leaders who may be more oriented toward peacemaking can assume power.

Ideally, aerial inspections can become a tool in larger peacemaking efforts when conditions are ripe for diplomatic settlement.[10] The role of aerial inspection in the peace treaty between

Egypt and Israel is the most prominent and complete example. But this level of commitment is not necessary in order to initiate aerial inspections. States may accept carefully circumscribed overflights as long as they conclude that their security posture will not be undermined by such operations. When viewed in terms of this minimal requirement, political consent need not be a significant hurdle, as long as procedures and safeguards associated with aerial inspections are carefully crafted and scrupulously followed.

In the context of the turbulent Middle East, the second condition for successful aerial inspections—positive command and control over military forces—is almost, if not equally, as important as the need for political consent at the highest levels of government. The consent of national leaders will be of little solace to pilots and inspectors if such leaders cannot guarantee the safety and security of the overflights. Unfortunately, a sad precedent already exists for this concern: nine Canadians were killed in 1974 when their UN aircraft was shot down by anti-aircraft fire in Syria.[11] Given the large number of missions that have thus far been flown in dangerous conditions in the Middle East, however, the overall safety record is good and suggests that a secure flight environment can be ensured.

To guard against a recurrence of unfortunate accidents, a clear mandate and guidelines for aerial inspections are essential. For example, the first Sinai disengagement agreement (Appendix I, Article V) expressly provided for the boundaries for aerial reconnaissance by Israel and Egypt (up to the median line of the buffer zone and up to the forward line of each party), flight path restrictions (a straight course along the median line of the buffer zone), six-hour prior notification of reconnaissance flights, specification of a four-hour window within which flights would be conducted, and designated days for each country's flights.[12] The second Sinai disengagement agreement expressly permitted the continuation of these procedures. Similar rules are in place governing the aerial inspection flights of the MFO over both Israel and the Sinai.

When slow-flying, third-party aerial inspections are carried out, the possibility of inadvertent accidents can be minimized if the inspection aircraft are distinctly colored and marked. Prior agreement on communications channels between the aircraft and the ground and prior notifications of overflights are essential to any aerial inspection regime.

A fourth condition bearing on aerial inspections concerns topography, which is quite suitable for such efforts in certain parts of the Middle East. The desert sands that distinguish part of the region, as in the Sinai, do not provide good cover for heavy military equipment or large organized units. Covert infiltration of units and equipment at night can become more difficult if inspection aircraft are able to fly at night equipped with infrared sensors that detect heat emissions.[13] Nevertheless, other areas of the Middle East, such as mist-covered valleys and mountainous regions, could pose difficulties for aerial inspectors, particularly if logistical problems have not been carefully addressed and if established ground rules do not permit the use of appropriate sensors.[14] Parts of southern Lebanon and the Golan Heights are cases in point and underscore the potential importance of complementary OSIs in many difficult settings.

Any overall discussion of preconditions for successful aerial inspections leads inevitably to the conclusion that political considerations are paramount. Aerial inspections are a tool to be used for agreed political purposes. As such, they cannot substitute for the political will to ease tensions across borders. When such will exists, however, aerial inspections can be a powerful instrument to prevent wars that arise from accidents or miscalculations and to assist peacemaking—as long as sound operational procedures and safeguards are in place.

In cases where these conditions have not been met, the results were predictably unsatisfactory. Despite heroic efforts by expert UN personnel, a number of operations in the Middle

East—especially the UN Interim Force in Lebanon (UNIFIL) in southern Lebanon and the UN Iran-Iraq Military Observer Group (UNIIMOG) along the Iran-Iraq border at the conclusion of their war—suffered from an inadequately drawn mandate and insufficient resources dedicated to aerial inspection requirements. For example, in UNIIMOG, the UN hoped to have twelve helicopters dedicated to border inspections, but both countries objected to the UN using its own resources for the task. The unsatisfactory compromise was the provision of six helicopters from each side, piloted by host nationals, with flight schedules completely under national control.

Such experiences raise the issue of whether third parties can reasonably carry out effective aerial inspections (or peacekeeping operations in general) if the parties themselves are less than fully dedicated to these tasks. The loosely drawn mandates for UNIFIL and UNIIMOG stand in sharp relief to those for the UN Disengagement Observer Force (UNDOF)—the Israeli-Syrian disengagement agreement—and for the MFO's oversight of the peace between Egypt and Israel. The latter accords were tightly constructed and have permitted these third-party peacekeeping operations to work quietly and effectively for years without major incidents.

When conditions are ripe for successful peacekeeping operations in the Middle East—when political will is solidly oriented toward a cessation of hostilities or a reduction in tensions, when command and control over forces in the field are strong, when clear operational rules have been agreed upon, and when the topography and financing are appropriate—conditions are also ripe for successful aerial inspections. Conversely, when conditions are not ripe for successful peacekeeping in the Middle East, aerial inspections can be extremely dangerous to crew members and can only be done unilaterally when one side dominates the skies, as with Israeli operations in southern Lebanon. Such flights, by definition, do not qualify as confidence building for both sides. Nor would inadequately conducted aerial inspections build confidence if gaps in coverage could be easily exploited.

Operational Considerations

Impartiality

If third parties are to conduct agreed aerial inspections, they need not be members of the neutral and nonaligned bloc of nations. Nor do they necessarily have to be neutral with respect to the degree of political affinity, economic ties, or even military support shown for the countries that have agreed to third-party overflights. As long as third parties have the confidence of all participating states to conduct overflights impartially they can succeed. Of course, third parties must demonstrate impartiality on all overflights to maintain the trust of the countries that have accepted aerial inspections. One way is to adhere rigorously to the same method of handling concerns over noncompliance regardless of the involved party. Another is to follow judiciously the same data reporting procedures for all parties. Impartiality can be reinforced by allowing liaison officers of the state overflown to accompany each third-party flight if there is sufficient room in the aircraft.

Symmetry

The most obvious way for third parties to demonstrate impartiality is to follow assiduously the principle of symmetry.[15] Symmetry need not require equal quotas of overflights if circumstances, such as the extent of geography to be covered or the number of prospective treaty-limited items in various zones, suggest otherwise. In other words, asymmetrical overflight requirements keyed to dissimilar constraints on force disposition are possible as long as they provide mutual benefits and do not lead to asymmetrical risks to the parties involved.

Nevertheless, symmetry with regard to overflight quotas has obvious political appeal. For this reason, asymmetrical geography might be addressed by negotiating equal quotas of aerial inspections of differing lengths. For example, since Israel is about one-fourth the size of Jordan, equal quotas of third-party overflights might permit missions over Jordan to be four times as long as missions over Israel. Symmetry is absolutely essential with respect to how the data collected by third parties are distributed to the countries overflown and the way with which concerns over compliance are dealt. The need for symmetry is no less essential when overflights are conducted by participating states in the region, either in conjunction with or in lieu of third-party aerial inspections.

Synergy

Like other monitoring tools, aerial inspections work best when they are used in conjunction with other measures and additional sources of information. In the context of peacemaking in the Middle East, the best example of synergistic monitoring approaches has been the Sinai disengagement agreements, which relied on aerial inspections in conjunction with nationally flown surveillance missions, multinational OSIs, and ground-based sensors to confirm data exchanges for demilitarized or thin-out zones.

Such synergy can work in several ways. Inspectors on the ground need information about where to best focus their investigations when large tracts of land are to be covered.

Aerial inspections can provide a synoptic view of the region to be covered, something inspectors on the ground are unable to do. The use of aircraft can thus help orient inspectors, as well as familiarize them with areas and facilities that will be the subject of OSIs.[16] In some cases, inspection aircraft might be employed to aid peacekeepers when they are faced with difficulties on the ground.

Aerial inspections before OSIs can help inspectors pinpoint new areas that require investigation and permit them to make the most efficient use of their time during site visits. This benefit was clearly evident in the second Sinai disengagement agreement, where the number of ground inspectors declined to 4,000 from the 7,000 authorized for the first disengagement agreement, even while the area to be inspected grew from less than 1,000 to almost 40,000 square kilometers.[17] Finally, third-party aerial inspections can provide a second opinion and reinforce the conclusions of other inspectors. For example, if a party such as Israel has less than full confidence in the impartiality of international inspectors, a cross-check by a credible third-party aerial inspection can have concrete utility in enhancing confidence.

Cost

Without adequate financing, aerial inspections are not feasible. In the Middle East, many states need not incur the considerable expense of purchasing new aircraft for this mission, as they already possess suitable platforms and sensors to carry out aerial inspections. Combat aircraft that have been equipped for reconnaissance missions and that pose no threat of offensive military action could be used, or small commercial aircraft could be employed, with modest modifications. For symbolic as well as other reasons, these options are inferior to using aircraft that connote confidence building rather than narrow military or civilian purposes. For third-party overflights, aircraft could be seconded from operational units stationed elsewhere. If based in the region, third-party aircraft should have distinctive markings for the aerial inspection mission. Additional costs would accrue from the operation and maintenance of these aircraft, as well as any data and image processing required.

Although some parties may balk at the costs, they are minimal when compared with the expense of carrying out combat operations. Thus, if states see value in aerial inspections and wish to avoid these far greater costs, they should be willing to pay appropriate shares of the "earnest" money associated with the inspections. The international community, which has such a vital stake in Middle East peace (as demonstrated in the Gulf War), also bears significant responsibility for helping fund those arrangements that may be critical to peacemaking in the region. Whether these costs should be assigned through the UN or on the basis of other arrangements, as with the MFO, is beyond the scope of this chapter. The point is that the inability of regional parties to fund the whole cost of peacekeeping arrangements such as aerial inspections should not and likely will not bar their employment, if their utility is clearly explained and clearly understood.

Logistics

Given the number of airfields, trained pilots, and maintenance personnel in the Middle East, the logistics of aerial inspections do not pose serious problems for many states in the region. In contrast, the logistics for third-party aerial inspections in the Middle East invariably pose certain problems, although not nearly so significant as the problems likely to be associated with gaining political consent for these missions. Put another way, if participating states in the Middle East have the will to accept aerial inspections, third parties will find a way to carry them out.

For example, third-party aircraft could be based in the region and rotated to all countries participating in aerial inspections. Despite the complications this practice would entail, it might prove necessary if participating states were to reserve the right to inspect the aircraft before overflights, based on stipulations that only specific types of sensors within agreed parameters be permitted on such overflights. Alternatively, third-party aircraft that are not terribly sophisticated could be based inside the region but not be subject to inspections by the states over whose territory they might fly. A third option would be to base more sophisticated aircraft outside the region, such as in Cyprus, with participating states foregoing inspections of the platform in lieu of constraints on flight paths, altitudes, and other safeguards, as discussed below.

Safeguards

The need for safeguards is directly proportional to the intrusiveness of the aerial inspection regime under consideration. Safeguards have been an important agenda item in the Open Skies talks and in the CFE negotiations because the anticipated overflights are quite far-ranging. To date, aerial inspections in the Middle East have not been precluded by disagreements over safeguards for at least two reasons. First, UN and MFO overflights have not carried sensors, relying instead on the eyes of the airborne inspectors aided by close passes, when needed.[18] Second, participating states appear to have agreed not to inspect U.S. reconnaissance aircraft that overfly the region along sensitive border regions. To date, all parties appear to be satisfied with receiving the same imagery or summary reports generated by such overflights.[19]

In the future, as in the past, a variety of safeguards are available for states willing to accept aerial inspections but wary of adding to their security concerns. For one thing, safeguards could be designed to relate to the platforms and sensors utilized, as well as to the operational practices employed on overflights.

Platforms

The size and characteristics of the aerial inspection platform will necessarily depend on the nature of the mission and the types of safeguards participating states deem essential. If the use of combat aircraft (or fighter aircraft that have been converted for reconnaissance missions) are barred by agreement, a wide range of platforms could be used, including small private or commercial jets (e.g., Gulfstreams or Cessnas) or larger transport aircraft modified to carry inspectors. If sensors were allowed, their weight and carriage could become factors in the choice of aircraft. More relevant for the sizing of the aircraft would be agreed procedures that required liaison officers from all participating states to accompany third-party inspectors. Procedures for periodic inspections of third-party aircraft could be agreed upon, if the participating states insisted on such inspections.

Sensors

If sensors were permitted on third-party aircraft based within the region, various safeguards could be employed to ease concerns over the data collected. To begin with, limitations on types of sensors and operating parameters could be negotiated. For example, using film cameras rather than electro-optical cameras might ease concerns about one side having a superior data processing capability. Restrictions on camera focal lengths and aircraft operating altitudes could also be negotiated to provide range limitations on the data collected. This approach could be applied to the choice of other sensors. Among the criteria for selection might be operability (including sensors that might be jointly operated), durability, and exportability to all participating states. As guiding principles, the sensors chosen would provide enough data for the mission at hand but not so much as to generate concerns over the collection of collateral intelligence or the generation of multiple false alarms.

If liaison officers from participating states were on board, constraints on sensor operations could be monitored during the mission. If the territory of two nations is to be overflown, three sets of each sensor could be carried on the aircraft; each state as well as the third party could randomly choose which sensor or data package to analyze. A simpler approach would have the third party responsible for providing the same data or summary analysis to all participating states, with periodic inspections of sensor pallets and aircraft to ensure that only agreed sensors are being flown. In theory, similar procedures could be worked out for third-party aircraft operating from bases outside the region, although this strategy might prove relatively difficult to implement. Alternatively, participating states might choose not to concern themselves with the sensors employed by a trusted third party, so long as they were confident of receiving the same data or summary reports.

Procedures

Operational procedures could be devised to allay concerns over the compromise of national security information. For example, as in the Sinai agreements, prenotification of overflights could be required, with a time frame sufficiently long to allow participating states to remove sensitive equipment from the field but too short for participating states to hide militarily significant violations of the accords. States or third parties conducting overflights might also be required to submit flight profile information, such as transit routes, flight lines and altitudes, and blocks of time within which the flights are to be conducted. If for some reason (such as mechanical difficulties or bad weather) an overflight could not take place within the time specified, it could be postponed in the interest of safety. If necessary, participating states could prohibit loitering, but allow "close looks" of agreed sites or installations. Other ideas developed from ongoing operations in the Middle East and in the Open Skies efforts could also be utilized.

New and Expanded Areas for Inspections

Border Security

Aerial inspection provisions that have worked successfully between Israel and its neighbors could also be employed in disputes between Arab states. If the government in Iraq, for example, wishes to demonstrate its peaceful intentions toward its neighbors, it could help alleviate concerns over border security by allowing aerial inspections under agreed procedures along Iraq's borders with Saudi Arabia, Kuwait, Jordan, Syria, Turkey, and Iran. The UN, which carried out aerial inspections along the Iran-Iraq border prior to the 1991 Persian Gulf War, could reconstitute and strengthen its operations there.

Short of formal agreement on third-party flights, substantial scope exists for the expanded use of informal or tacit arrangements that allow each side's specially equipped aircraft to fly alongside border areas in the Gulf.[20] States that have demonstrated good faith efforts to reduce tensions and engage in peacemaking, which now lack the technical means to undertake such flights, might be encouraged to institute them and to develop a framework of understanding on their use.

As is done elsewhere in the region, these flights could be undertaken by aircraft of participating states as well as by third-party aircraft based inside or outside the region. Third-party flights along national borders—perhaps under the auspices of the Arab League and of the Gulf Cooperation Council—could have important symbolic value, as they might underscore multinational interest in maintaining peace between Iraq and its neighbors. Safeguards against the misuse of the information acquired on overflights would be essential. Perhaps overflights could be undertaken without the use of sensors, as is currently the case with UN peacekeeping missions in the region.

If the Iraqi government did not wish to expressly permit cooperative aerial inspections, states in the region as well as third parties currently have the option to carry inspections out unilaterally along Iraq's borders. These flights could provide important indications and warning of military buildups, focusing diplomatic efforts on reducing tensions and making it harder for political leaders in the region to deny troubling developments. Unilateral flights of this kind, however, would not qualify as a CBM in the strict sense of the term.

Zones of Limitation

Border security aerial inspections will not generate confidence in security if they reveal large concentrations of opposing forces nearby. As a result, states may wish to reaffirm national borders by agreeing to limitations on the extent and disposition of military manpower or equipment behind them. As in the case of the Sinai disengagement agreements, aerial and ground inspections can help confirm agreed limitations on the number of personnel and associated equipment in sensitive regions. Over time, expanded thin-out zones could be negotiated if states were so inclined. Thin-out zones need not be symmetrical to increase confidence between states, as long as agreed arrangements served common security objectives. Such agreements could help stabilize the Iran-Iraq border, as well as the borders between Iraq and Kuwait and Saudi Arabia. Thin-out zones could be monitored by third-party aircraft based within or outside of the region.

Exclusion or Demilitarized Zones

Another way for states in the Middle East to build confidence in the region would be to accept exclusion or demilitarized zones for specific kinds of weapons systems. Such zones could be characterized as steps toward the ultimate goal of eliminating all weapons with particular characteristics from the region.

For example, states wishing to associate themselves with the objective of eliminating the threat posed by medium-range ballistic missiles might begin by designating exclusion zones for such weapons within the region. Wherever possible, these zones would be configured in such a way to protect large cities in the region against the threat of weapons of mass destruction carried by ballistic missiles. These zones could be monitored by NTM possessed by states outside the region, with assessments provided to all participating states. Third-party and national aerial inspections could also be carried out to confirm exclusion or demilitarized zones.

In any of the negotiated outcomes to the Palestinian question (except the status quo), Israel will almost certainly insist on a virtual demilitarization of the West Bank and Gaza, except for security points held by the Israeli military. Should such conditions ultimately be accepted by Palestinian leaders, one can envisage the construction of an effective combination of aerial and ground inspections conducted by mutually agreed third parties or by joint Palestinian-Israeli patrols.

Similarly, any agreements reached on force dispositions between Israel and Syria, Jordan, or Lebanon as elements of a peace treaty will require verification. Aerial inspection carried out openly by a regionally based third party or discreetly from outside the region would play a key part in making such agreements possible and credible. To the extent that all sides could also agree to on-site inspection, the accords would be that much stronger and their credibility would be enhanced.

Monitoring Facilities of Special Interest

Attempts to negotiate a nuclear and chemical weapons free zone in the Middle East face many hurdles. One place to begin this arduous process is to demonstrate that facilities suspected of producing special nuclear materials for use in nuclear weapons, or facilities suspected of involvement in producing chemical weapons, have been deactivated or are not currently engaged in such activities.

An ideal way to demonstrate that suspected facilities are not engaged in troubling activities is through OSIs. But states in the region are unlikely to permit such inspections, given the existing levels of distrust and the sensitivity of the facilities of interest. If the activities in question are not heavily and effectively shielded, their deactivation could be monitored by aircraft employing sensors to observe heat emissions.[21] In this way, remote confirmation of the shut-down of ground-level facilities at Dimona, for example, might be accomplished, as has been suggested by a 1990 UN study on the establishment of a nuclear weapons free zone in the Middle East.[22] Steps taken to deactivate facilities suspected of chemical weapons production could also be monitored by such overflights, perhaps by third-party aircraft following agreed procedures.

Conclusion

The Middle East has known far more war fighting than peacemaking. One way to strengthen diplomacy and make the resort to war in the region less likely is for peacemakers to use an essential instrument of military operations—reconnaissance aircraft. Carefully circumscribed aerial inspections have already been employed in the region to help confirm demilitarized and thin-out zones and establish a few relatively quiet borders. When conditions are in place for successful aerial overflights, and with proper appreciation for operational considerations and safeguards, cooperative aerial inspections could become a powerful instrument for peace in the Middle East. The time is appropriate to build on the successful record of the past decade and a half, and to further investigate ways in which this proven technique could be used elsewhere in the region.

4. Arms Control and the Proliferation of Ballistic Missiles

W. Seth Carus and Janne E. Nolan

The multinational conflict with Iraq, underscored by dramatic scenes of Iraqi Scud missiles attacking population centers in Israel and Saudi Arabia, focused the world's attention on the problems posed by the global spread of ballistic missiles. Even as efforts proceeded to implement the terms of UN Security Council Resolution 687, the blueprint for the disarmament of Iraq, missile programs were continuing in many other countries throughout the Third World.

The proliferation of ballistic missiles is posing a particular challenge to the prospects for achieving peace and stability in the Middle East. Every significant military power in the region has a missile force, and some of these already are quite advanced. Despite severe resource constraints in other areas, the level of investment being devoted to national missile programs is increasing, gradually adding to the size and capabilities of deployed missile forces among major regional antagonists. For all their operational limitations, Iraqi Scud missile strikes during the Persian Gulf War seem to have encouraged countries to redouble efforts to acquire new and more capable systems, either through indigenous development programs or through purchases from outside suppliers.[1]

This trend seems to indicate the growing importance of ballistic missiles in the military doctrines of countries in the region.

During the Iran-Iraq War in the 1980s, for example, both Iran and Iraq treated their ballistic missiles as central to their military strategy—the limited accuracy and payload of both sides' missile arsenals notwithstanding. The point was driven home again by Iraq's missile attacks on Israel and Saudi Arabia during the Persian Gulf War. Although they lacked the ability to target accurately, Iraqi missile strikes extended the battlefield and threatened to undercut the multinational coalition by trying to pressure Israel to retaliate.

Barring significant alterations in the regional security environment, one must assume that surface-to-surface missiles will become even more important in future conflicts, with both regional and international security implications. This chapter provides an overview of the current status of missile arsenals in the Middle East, assesses the motivations underlying the acquisition of missiles among major regional actors, and analyzes the extent to which arms control negotiations, confidence-building measures (CBMs), and other policy instruments could be useful in the Middle Eastern context.

Overview of Missile Forces

Eight Middle Eastern countries currently possess ballistic missiles: Egypt, Iran, Iraq, Israel, Libya, Saudi Arabia, Syria, and Yemen.[2] Several have used their missiles during four different conflicts.[3] Five have indigenous missile development programs, including Egypt, Iran, Iraq, Israel, and Libya. A sixth, Syria, lacks the ability to produce missiles but was able to enhance the capabilities of foreign-supplied systems by giving them new kinds of warheads.[4]

The pattern of missile development among countries varies widely, requiring a case-by-case review of their missile programs as a necessary point of departure.

Egypt

The genesis of Egyptian interest in ballistic missiles dates back to the late 1950s when Egypt organized a ballistic missile development program using technical assistance from West Germany. Despite considerable investment over several years, the program failed and was terminated in the early 1960s. In the early 1970s Egypt turned instead to the Soviet Union to acquire FROG rockets and Scud surface-to-surface missiles. Egypt used both these systems during the 1973 Arab-Israeli War, including at least three Scud missile strikes and perhaps more than 100 FROGs launched against Israeli targets in the Sinai. The rockets and missiles were employed in deep strike attacks against military targets in rear areas, including air bases and command posts.

Following the 1973 war, Egypt resumed missile development activities, albeit on a smaller scale. Efforts were made to master Scud technology as part of a cooperative program with North Korea. Egypt is believed to have provided copies of the Scud to North Korea in the late 1970s, which helped the latter achieve considerable proficiency in Scud missile development a decade later.

Egypt began much-expanded missile development efforts in the early 1980s. After the outbreak of the Iran-Iraq War, several joint projects with Iraq were initiated. The most significant of these was the Condor 2 missile project, a joint Iraqi-Argentinian-Egyptian effort to develop a medium-range ballistic missile. Egyptian officials negotiated the terms of the Condor agreement with Argentina in 1984 and apparently agreed to serve as a conduit for technology flows to Iraq, which provided major financing for the project until 1988. The program was terminated in 1990, apparently due to financial constraints and political pressures brought by the United States against Argentina.

In addition, Egypt may have assisted Iraq in developing the extended-range Al-Hussein missile during the mid-1980s and did develop the Saqr-80, a replacement for the FROG-7 rocket, in a cooperative project with French companies.

Iran

Prompted by the threat of Iraqi missile attacks during the Persian Gulf War, Iran acquired its first ballistic missiles in 1985, when it received about 30 Scud-Bs from Libya.[5] At about the same time, Iran also negotiated a deal for Scud missiles with North Korea. The Iranians provided the funding needed to complete development of a North Korean copy of the Scud-B, and North Korea apparently agreed to help Iran develop its own Scud production capability. Iran reportedly received 100 North Korean Scuds between 1987 and 1988. North Korea is now believed to have upgraded the capability of the Scud-B, extending its range to between 372 and 558 miles and improving its accuracy. The latter system, commonly referred to as Scud-C, has reportedly been sold in recent months to Syria as well as to Iran.

The Iranians also claim to be domestically producing a missile with a range of 200 kilometers and several long-range artillery rockets, including the Oghab, with a range of 40 kilometers, and the Nazeat, with a 90-kilometer range. In addition, the Iranians have been trying to develop an indigenous solid-fuel missile capability, perhaps relying on technical assistance from China. Iran is reported to have purchased Chinese M-9 missiles as well, which have a longer range than any missile currently in Iran's inventory. And there are reports that Iran is attempting to develop chemical warheads for its missile forces.

Despite the short range of Iranian Scud-B missiles and Oghab rockets, both were used extensively against Iraq in the last phases of the Iran-Iraq War. Many cities near the border between the two countries were attacked. These strikes were a significant element of Iranian strategy against Iraq, helping to compensate for the absence of an effective air force.

Iraq

Before the military conflict resulting from Iraq's invasion of Kuwait, Iraq had the most ambitious missile program in the region. It also has made the most extensive use of short- and medium-range ballistic missiles in actual military operations of any country in the Middle East. In addition to the large number of ballistic missiles Iraq fired during the Iran-Iraq War, Iraq demonstrated its reliance on missiles during its confrontation with the U.S.-led coalition in the Persian Gulf War, launching at least eighty-one modified Scud Al-Hussein missiles at targets in Israel and Saudi Arabia over the course of the conflict.

The Iraqis had at least six different missile programs before the war. The most advanced was the Al-Hussein missile, based on Soviet-supplied Scud-Bs, first used in 1988 and again in 1991. Iraq simultaneously attempted to produce completely new types of the extended-range Scud, apparently relying on components manufactured in several western countries, including West Germany. The Iraqis made considerable progress in this program before the crisis over Kuwait erupted in August 1990, including the development and testing of a nuclear-capable medium-range ballistic missile. Iraq also hoped to develop much longer range missiles, with ranges up to 2,000 kilometers.

The Iraqis made various other claims about their missile production capabilities before the war, including that they were converting some of their Soviet-supplied SA-2 and SA-3 surface-to-air missiles to a surface-to-surface mode. In addition, Iraq attempted to develop an antitactical ballistic missile, the Fao. Finally, Iraq has had several long-range artillery rocket programs, such as versions of the Brazilian ASTROS II (ranges of up to 60 kilometers) built under license, the Ababil rockets with ranges of 50 and 100 kilometers (based on a Yugoslav design), and an indigenous version of the Soviet FROG-7 known as the Laith 90, with a range of 90 kilometers.

The scope of Iraq's defense industrial ambitions began to be revealed in detail in late 1991 as a result of UN efforts to implement Resolution 687. In conjunction with nuclear and chemical weapons programs, the Iraqi technical infrastructure established to produce missiles was revealed to be even more extensive than had been thought among western experts. In addition to the numerous missile programs, Iraq also was involved in Project Babylon, an effort to produce long-range guns that had ranges of hundreds of kilometers, potentially equipped to carry nuclear and chemical ordnance. The future status of all of Iraq's weapons programs will depend on the UN's success in implementing and enforcing Resolution 687.

Israel

Israel is widely believed to have the most advanced missile program in the Middle East. Little about the program has been officially confirmed—the Israeli government has never admitted to possessing an indigenously produced ballistic missile, let alone a deployed force. Israeli missile development efforts date back roughly thirty years. Initially, these efforts involved a contract with France, under the so-called MD-620 and MD-660 missile programs, in which missiles were developed in France for transfer to Israel. Following the rupture of the Israeli-French arms relationship in the late 1960s, however, the production effort was transferred to Israel.

It appears that Israel has developed several generations of missiles, commonly known in the West as Jericho I, Jericho II, and Jericho IIB. Deployed versions are reported to have ranges of roughly 450 kilometers, 800 kilometers, and 1,500 kilometers, respectively. Israel may be attempting to develop systems with even longer ranges, including a system based on the Shavit space launch vehicle, which was first tested in the mid-1980s.

Israel is believed to have succeeded in developing and deploying missiles for nuclear delivery. In addition, Israel also has shown interest in conventionally armed missiles for tactical missions. Two hundred Lance missiles armed with cluster munitions warheads were acquired from the United States during the 1970s. These are probably now second-line systems, given Israeli development of more advanced long-range artillery rockets with comparable ranges, such as the ninety-kilometer-range MAR-350. Israel also has shown considerable interest in land-attack cruise missiles. Its inventory is known to include long-endurance kamikaze drones, intended mainly to attack electronic systems. Further, Israel has indicated interest in developing systems capable of attacking an even broader range of targets with advanced conventional munitions.

Libya

The Soviet Union is believed to have supplied eighty Scud-B and forty FROG 7 launchers to Libya since the 1970s, providing the Libyans with a missile force disproportionately large for a country of its size. In addition, it appears that Libya tried to purchase missiles from China and North Korea in the late 1980s.[6]

The Libyans have also attempted to develop their own missiles, but with limited success. During the late 1970s and early 1980s, a firm owned by the Swedish government offered training in missile guidance techniques to Libyan engineers.[7] Later, a West German space launcher development firm, OTRAG, located its facilities in Libya. Although the company eventually pulled out of Libya, a group of German engineers associated with the project apparently remained in the country, working on a project known as Al Fateh.

The Libyans have tried to buy missile technology from other foreign sources. In early 1988, for example, Libya attempted to negotiate a multi-billion dollar deal with a Brazilian missile company to develop and coproduce a missile with a range of 1,000 kilometers. Nothing apparently came of the attempt.[8]

Saudi Arabia

Apparently in response Israel's acquisition of Lance missiles, Saudi Arabia attempted to acquire this system from the United States in the late 1970s. The United States rejected the Saudi request, and subsequent requests to obtain the missile in the early 1980s also were denied.

In mid-1985 the Saudis asked the Chinese for their DF-3A medium-range ballistic missile. It is possible that Saudi interest in acquiring a missile was intensified by the Iranian acquisition of Scud missiles and the use of those missiles against Baghdad. Some sources suggest that the Chinese initially offered the Saudis the M-9 missile, then in the early stages of development, but that the Saudis declined the offer, wanting instead to acquire a missile force as quickly as possible. The M-9 was not going to be available until the end of the decade at the earliest, so the Chinese sold the DF-3A missile in its place. Developed in the late 1960s, the DF-3A is a nuclear-capable missile with a range of about 2,600 kilometers. The Saudi DF-3A missiles were equipped only with conventional warheads, however, which may reduce the missile's effective range by adding to its weight.

It has been reported in recent months that the Saudis were considering acquiring the U.S. Army ATACMS, a conventionally armed missile with a range of about 150 kilometers. This system is fired from the same launcher as the thirty-kilometer-range MLRS artillery rocket. Successful employment of the ATACMS by the U.S. Army against Iraqi targets has apparently increased Saudi interest in this weapon, although the United States has not yet approved such a sale.

Syria

The Syrian military acquired its first Soviet FROG-7 surface-to-surface rockets just before the 1973 Arab-Israeli War. About twenty-five of these rockets were fired at Israeli targets during the fighting, including attacks on at least two air bases. Although the effectiveness of the rockets was quite limited, the Syrians were sufficiently impressed with the potential of these weapons to subsequently acquire Scud-B and SS-21 missiles, again from the Soviet Union.

In addition, the Syrians have attempted to acquire medium-range missiles. Efforts were made to purchase SS-23 missiles from the Soviet Union in the late 1980s, but the requests were rejected. Subsequently, Syria tried to obtain Chinese-made M-9 missiles. Pressure from the United States first appeared to have convinced the Chinese to turn down the request, but reports persist that Syria has obtained either the M-9 or the 300-kilometer-range M-11 from China.

In early 1991, Syria reportedly took delivery of extended-range Scud missiles built in North Korea and continues to purchase Scud-related equipment from the Koreans. These missiles are believed to have a range of 450 kilometers. In addition, Syria may have recently ordered more SS-21 short-range ballistic missiles from Moscow as part of a larger arms purchase package, although this transaction has not been confirmed.

Syria is reported to have developed chemical warheads for its Scud-B missiles. These weapons are intended to challenge the superiority of Israeli conventional and nuclear capabilities. In theory, the threat of chemical retaliation could make it possible for Syria to limit Israeli conventional escalation in a conflict by providing it with a form of retaliation that it previously lacked. Similarly, chemical weapons could provide a limited deterrence against an Israeli nuclear strike. At the very least, chemical warheads ensure that Israel has reason to fear that use of its nuclear forces could result in chemical weapons attacks against its population.

Yemen

Although less is known of Yemen's missile forces compared with other regional arsenals, both North Yemen and South

Yemen had acquired missile capabilities by purchasing Soviet systems before the two countries merged. North Yemen is believed to have acquired SS-21 missiles, and South Yemen had FROG-7 and Scud-B missiles. Yemen has no missile production capabilities, and its limited missile arsenal appears to be largely symbolic.

Motivations Underlying Missile Programs

The motivations driving different countries in the Middle East to acquire ballistic missiles vary according to the countries' military priorities, threat perceptions, and relative commitment to defense industrial development. In some cases, the primary factor for acquiring missiles appears to be prestige. Missiles are symbols of modernity and sovereignty, believed to enhance the regional or international status of the country possessing them. This situation appears to be the case particularly in Yemen and Libya, where the capabilities of their current missile forces are so limited that the missiles are of far greater political than military significance. The earlier phases of the Egyptian missile program under President Nasser seem to have been motivated largely by prestige as well. Nasser repeatedly expressed the desire to demonstrate Egypt's growing technological prowess, even when the costs of the investment outweighed the calculable military utility of the systems under development.

Egyptian motivations seem to have evolved in the 1970s. The employment of rockets and missiles during the 1973 war points to the importance of operational military considerations, while the character of the new Saqr-80 rocket tends to reinforce the view that the Egyptian military now assigns an important role to achieving the capability to fire into enemy rear areas from long ranges.

Although prestige factors may play a role in the decision-making of some countries, the majority of Middle Eastern ballistic missile forces appear to have direct strategic or tactical significance. In some cases, ballistic missiles have been acquired to overcome inferiority in other areas of military capacity, often as compensation for inadequacies of air power. Given the relative weakness of the Syrian air force compared with that of Israel, for example, missile operations have assumed a central role in Syrian military doctrine. From a Syrian perspective, medium-range missiles make it possible to attack targets in central Israel from positions deep inside Syria, where the missile launchers would be less vulnerable to air attacks than attacks on aircraft. Other countries, including Iraq, seem to have similar notions of the utility of missiles, a perception that must have been reinforced by the Persian Gulf War. Well after the Iraqi air force was crippled by the coalition's air strikes, Scud missiles fired from mobile launchers continued to elude detection and destruction.

Other states, especially Saudi Arabia, Israel, and even Iran, seem to view their missile arsenals more as part of a deterrent strategy. Iranian officials claim their missile program is a deterrent against Iraqi missile strikes.[9] Saudi officials, likewise, have always claimed that their Chinese-origin missiles were acquired as a deterrent against potential Iranian missile strikes, although events during the 1991 Persian Gulf War cast considerable doubt on the deterrent value of these missiles.[10] Israeli interest in a modern missile force also has been tied to its efforts to develop a credible nuclear and advanced conventional deterrent against the quantitative superiority of its Arab antagonists.[11] The combination of nuclear weapons and prompt delivery systems guarantees Israel an absolute retaliatory capability against any act of aggression.

The importance countries ascribe to their missile forces is a vital consideration in devising arms control policies. Convincing countries to reduce their reliance on ballistic missile forces may not be possible without commensurate adjustments in the other military capabilities of their opponents, especially air power. For some countries, including Israel, the development of advanced systems such as missiles is also valued as a means to advance overall technological and military independence. Until such domestic factors are taken more fully into account, controls on the demand for missiles will be difficult to achieve.

Assessing the Prospects for Arms Control

Three approaches traditionally have guided efforts to control missile forces, largely derived from the experience of NATO-Warsaw Pact negotiations. The most common approach is to try to impose quantitative and, less frequently, qualitative constraints on missiles. Arms control agreements dating back to SALT I contain many such provisions, including ceilings on numbers of deployed systems or restrictions on the development of new missile types.

The second approach tries to place limits on the way states deploy missiles and conduct operations. Such constraints were at the heart of the negotiations that helped end the Cuban Missile Crisis in 1962, for example, and figured prominently in U.S.-Soviet agreements to reduce the risk of inadvertent nuclear war. In addition to geographical constraints on where missiles can be deployed, such as the 1967 Outer Space Treaty, agreements can include measures to provide advance warning of planned missile test launches or for secure communication links between adversaries for crisis management.

Recently, the United States and the Soviet Union adopted a new approach, agreeing to eliminate entire categories of missiles under strict verification procedures, as in the INF Treaty, and by parallel unilateral initiatives, as were proposed separately by Presidents Bush and Gorbachev in 1991 for eliminating short-range nuclear forces.[12]

No existing treaties limit missile capabilities outside the East-West context, and none is currently under negotiation. In devising such policy for new regions, one must be sensitive to some of the potential limitations of technical arms control instruments for stemming regional missile proliferation. The applicability of some of these policies may be impeded by the following considerations:

- The relatively abstract nature of the East-West military competition is different from the diffuse and highly volatile political-military conditions that exist in the countries of the Middle East where missile proliferation is currently of most concern. Shifting alliances, disputed borders, and intractable patterns of enmity, often based on ethnic or religious antagonisms of centuries' duration—these all defy uniform, technical approaches.
- It was commonly understood among NATO and Warsaw Pact nations during the Cold War that the main objective of nuclear weapons was that they never be used. In contrast, many of the regional adversaries in the Middle East want to acquire ballistic missiles specifically to prosecute potential military conflicts more effectively.
- The United States and the Soviet Union had several decades to develop the enabling agreements and technical foundations for reaching accommodation about nuclear and, more recently, conventional forces. The difficulties associated with defining the conventional balance in the European theater suggest the formidable challenges in defining regional limitations in the Middle East, for which there is not yet even a rudimentary framework for common agreement.
- Agreed ceilings on the numbers of particular types of weapons, the mainstay of strategic force reductions, presuppose that one can at least roughly calculate equivalencies in weapons types, and agree that lower levels of such weapons are a step towards enhancing stability. The definition of desirable limits derives from a common understanding of what is needed to achieve overall military stability, the conditions for which must

be within reach. But in the Middle East, Israel counts the inventories of the Arab and Persian Gulf states as a collective threat to its security, and thus pursues qualitative superiority to offset these states' numerical superiority in conventional weaponry and military manpower. The Arab states, on the other hand, consider Israel's nuclear and missile capabilities to outweigh their superiority in numbers, and thus seek comparable qualitative capabilities to offset what they perceive as the Israeli threat.

- Patterns of regional enmity also supersede traditional territorial boundaries in the Middle East, further complicating the delineation of a regional framework suitable for negotiations. Saudi Arabia, for instance, considers both Iran and Israel regional threats. The basis for defining coherent regions, let alone for developing common concepts of stability, eludes current political-military realities.

- Even more than strategic arms control, negotiated limitations on regional arsenals depend on a measure of political accommodation among adversaries that does not exist in regions where missile proliferation is most problematic. Many countries in the Middle East do not share the developed world's concerns about the importance of missile restraint. Efforts to discourage their military ambitions, especially through the denial of exports, is often seen as discriminatory. Diplomatic denunciations of the legitimacy of ballistic missiles (and chemical and nuclear weapons) often incur jaundiced accusations of hypocrisy from countries whose fledgling military arsenals are dwarfed by those of the superpowers.

   In light of these complexities, attempting to negotiate or impose technical limitations on regional arsenals—such as numerical ceilings on missiles and warheads or constraints on the ranges of missiles, for example—seems not to be a promising approach to containing the threat of ballistic missiles.

CSBMs—instruments that do not affect the size or capabilities of forces per se but are aimed at increasing communications between adversaries—would appear by contrast to have far more likelihood of success in the near term. CSBMs may be particularly appropriate in situations where there are disparities in military balance, diffuse zones of dispute, and limited foundations for political accommodation. As one analyst summarized it, "A particular value of confidence-building measures is that their negotiation can bypass questions of relative military capabilities, where problems of quantification, verification, and asymmetrical perceptions of threat can bog down discussions. Confidence-building measures aim directly at assessments of intent, regardless of capabilities."[15] Examining the reasons why concrete technical arms control efforts will be difficult in the Middle East helps to illuminate some of the variables that will have to be considered in developing workable missile restraint policies for this region.

Evaluating Missile Arms Control Proposals

Regional Bans on Ballistic Missiles

Several proposals have been advanced to ban the purchase, production, and testing of ballistic missiles in the Middle East, including one from President Bush in May 1991. The most comprehensive version appeared in a 1990 report of the UN secretary-general on the "Establishment of a Nuclear-Weapon-Free Zone in the Region of the Middle East," which suggested that a freeze on additional deployments of ballistic missiles could ease tensions in the region. The authors of the report said, "As a starting point for discussions, it would be desirable to consider a complete suspension by all states in the region of domestic production and of imports of missiles beyond a certain range."[14]

According to this conception, no attempt would be made to control missile research and development, although flight testing would be prohibited in an effort to constrain the deployment of new generations of missiles. Missiles defined as "battlefield range" would not be covered, and existing inventories would not be subject to elimination. The authors of the UN report admit that small-scale violations of the production and import freeze could take place, but argue that even a relatively simple verification scheme would be enough to detect substantial violations that could be considered militarily significant.

In early 1991 the U.S. government began to consider a ban on the development and acquisition of surface-to-surface missiles for the Middle East. On May 29, 1991, President Bush announced a Middle East arms control initiative that included some elements aimed specifically at surface-to-surface missiles. For example, the initiative proposes a freeze on the acquisition, production, and testing of surface-to-surface missiles by states in the Middle East with a view to the ultimate elimination of such missiles from their national arsenals. Suppliers would also step up efforts to coordinate export licensing for equipment technology and services that could be used to manufacture surface-to-surface missiles. Export licenses would be provided only to peaceful end users.[15]

The exact scope of the Bush proposal is unclear. For example, a surface-to-surface missile could be taken to include short-range tactical weapons, such as antitank weapons, as well as long-range systems such as the Scud-B and the Israeli Jericho missile. It appears that the proposal would cover ground-launched cruise missiles, but probably not those fired from aircraft. Further, whether long-range artillery rockets such as the FROG-7, with a range of seventy kilometers, would be banned is unclear.

The ambiguity of the Bush proposal was complicated in the subsequent July 1991 meeting held in Paris among the world's five major arms suppliers to discuss arms sales policies. The participants issued a joint communiqué calling for the establishment of "a weapons of mass destruction–free zone in the Middle East" (July 11). This included a ban on "ground-to-ground missiles." The shift in language from "surface-to-surface" missiles, as originally advocated by the United States, had some significant substantive implications. The new formulation appears intended to exclude antiship missiles, whether fired from ships or land-based launchers. However, the original U.S. proposal probably would have banned ship-launched attack missiles, which would seemingly be allowed under the revised language aimed specifically at ground-launched weapons.

For all its obvious merits, a regional missile freeze would face several challenges that would have to be dealt with and overcome before such an effort could be successfully implemented. First, there is not now a firm commitment among the Big Five arms suppliers, let alone other arms exporters, to cease exports of missiles and missile-related technologies to the Middle East. China, for one, continues to resist the notion that ballistic missiles and their components should be subject to stricter export prohibitions than are applied to other delivery systems. To be viable, a missile freeze obviously would require support from a large number of countries. China aside, North Korea, Brazil, and Argentina could undercut a missile freeze with their own production programs, albeit with less-advanced technologies than are available in the West. To elicit compliance, the United States and its partners will have to give a lot more thought to the kinds of incentives they are prepared to offer, including perhaps access to other kinds of advanced weaponry, as well as enforcement mechanisms, including punitive sanctions on violators.

Second, it is not clear what would be covered by the ban. A considerable number of short-range tactical weapons could be considered "surface-to-surface" or "ground-to-ground" missiles. For example, an antitank missile like the TOW missile, which has a range of only 3,750 meters, could be covered by such language. Moreover, longer-range systems, such as Israel's Harpy kamikaze antiradiation missile, also would be banned, even though it is intended only to attack radars and similar electronic systems. Moreover, whether unguided weapons, such as artillery rockets, would be banned is unclear. Normally, the "missile" category is intended to cover only guided weapons, suggesting that long-range artillery rockets with large warheads would be permissible, while other weapons with shorter ranges and smaller warheads would be banned.[16]

A missile freeze also would have to contend with the proliferation of cruise missiles and with defensive systems, such as Patriot or the emerging U.S.-Israeli Arrow program. Several Middle East countries already possess antiship cruise missiles with ranges of up to 200 kilometers. Many of those weapons could be converted into land-attack weapons, as the United States did with a version of its Harpoon antiship missile.[17] It is possible that Israel already has long-range land-attack cruise missiles.[18] With respect to surface-to-air missiles, a number of anti-aircraft systems can be adapted with relatively little difficulty to surface-to-surface roles, as has occurred in a number of instances.[19]

Third, the missile freeze proposal provides no guidance on how to deal with indigenous missile development programs, or how a ban would affect local producers in the near or long term. What would be done about disparities in existing missile arsenals and production capabilities and the degree to which current imbalances in missile inventories could prove destabilizing are vital issues that have yet to be debated. Indeed, it is not clear how a ban on industrial countries' ballistic missile exports will evolve into a regional initiative, nor how such an initiative would be negotiated or verified.

But if local states were to become engaged in a process that led to a missile ban, such an agreement could help reduce regional tensions significantly. Israel's security certainly would be easier to guarantee in an environment in which Iraq, Syria, and other antagonists were not continuing to modernize their missile forces. By removing an element of the regional arms competition that puts a special premium on the ability to launch prompt, preemptive attacks, regional tensions and even the pace of overall military acquisitions might be substantially reduced. Moreover, in an environment of constrained offensive missile forces, the deployment of defensive systems by mutual consent also might be a stabilizing measure.

A ban on missiles also would be far easier to verify than a negotiated effort to restrict ranges or numbers. The effectiveness or importance of numerical ceilings on missiles in these volatile regions is questionable. As was demonstrated in the 1988 War of the Cities and again in the Persian Gulf War, even small numbers of missiles can devastate civilian targets, and the missiles could be even more lethal if armed with nonconventional munitions.

A Middle East INF Treaty

Several analysts have suggested that it might be possible to adapt the U.S.-Soviet 1986 Treaty on Intermediate Nuclear Forces (INF) Treaty to the Middle East.[20] The INF Treaty eliminated all intermediate-range missiles, defined as those having ranges between 1,000 and 5,500 kilometers, and shorter-range systems, defined as having ranges between 500 and 1,000 kilometers. Only ballistic and cruise missiles fired from ground launchers are included. The treaty does not prohibit either intercontinental ballistic missiles with ranges of more than 5,500 kilometers or short-range ballistic missiles with ranges of less than 500 kilometers. The treaty also does not limit air- or sea-launched missile systems.

A Middle East INF treaty would have certain advantages. The moderate Arab states would benefit from the elimination of Israeli intermediate-range missiles and by precluding Iran and Iraq from obtaining such weapons. In addition, the missile threat posed among Arab states engaged in inter-Arab antagonisms—such as Syria and Lebanon, Saudi Arabia and Iraq, and Iraq and Iran—would be severely diminished. For Israel, such an agreement would eliminate missiles in service or under development in Arab countries, including Iraq and Saudi Arabia, that could target deep into Israeli territory.

A regional INF agreement also would have the advantage of already having adherence to its terms by the United States and the former Soviet Union, which have foresworn this category of weaponry. With recent U.S.-Soviet initiatives to eliminate shorter-range systems as well, the basis for a global ban on all missiles falling below 5,500 kilometers also might be desirable. Such an agreement would require the support of other missile powers, including France, China, and possibly India.

The benefits of INF-type range constraints on missiles, however, would not be equitably distributed among the countries in the region. Geography ensures that the significance of range limits varies considerably from one country to the next. As was illustrated in the Iran-Iraq War, for example, most Iraqi cities are within 300 kilometers of the border with Iran, while the eastern limits of Baghdad are only about 130 kilometers from Iranian territory. Iran needed only Scud-B missiles to hit targets throughout Iraqi territory, while its nascent 200-kilometer-range missiles could reach a large number of strategic locations. Considerably longer ranges are needed for Iraqi missiles to hit comparable targets in Iran. Scud-B missiles were capable of striking cities only in the western parts of Iran, and a number of strategically important cities, including Qom and Tehran, were well out of range of the Scud-B. Even after Iraq developed its Al-Hussein missile, many Iranian cities remained out of range of Iraq's missiles.

The experience of the Persian Gulf War demonstrates that missiles based in western Iraq were capable of hitting targets in Israel, because less than 600 kilometers separates potential launch sites in western Iraq from key Israeli cities. Indeed, the western border of Iraq is less than 400 kilometers from Tel Aviv. Because Iraq's western part is largely uninhabited, there are few strategic targets in that part of the country. A retaliating Israeli missile would need a range of about 800 kilometers to reach Baghdad.

As these figures suggest, a 500-kilometer range limitation on Israeli forces would eliminate missiles it could use against Iraq. Only if the limit were lowered to 300 kilometers would both countries lose the ability to target one another with missile strikes.

As the prohibited range of systems is reduced to lower levels, however, a larger number of more varied systems would have to be taken into account, making the technical difficulties of implementing and verifying an INF-type agreement in the Middle East more acute. In order to have confidence in the compliance of the treaty signatories, intelligence capabilities would have to be vastly improved. The level of intelligence information about regional missile arsenals to date has not been adequate to suggest a strong foundation for such an ambitious undertaking. Iraq's ability to fire Al-Hussein missiles at Tehran and other cities deep in Iran in the 1980s, for example, was a major intelligence surprise.[21] And although it is perhaps understandable that the United States (and others) underestimated Iraqi capabilities in late 1987 and early 1988, the reasons for similar intelligence failures in 1991 were not so clear. It appears that the scope of the threat posed by Iraqi missiles to the U.S.-led coalition was grossly underestimated; as a result, substantial numbers of aircraft had to be diverted to hunt for Iraq's mobile missile launchers, with extremely limited success.

Given the state of missiles already in the Middle East, moreover, the negotiation of equitable range limitations that are militarily meaningful would be difficult. Inventories in Israel and Saudi Arabia (and in Iraq before the Persian Gulf War) contain missiles whose ranges are well beyond what could be considered acceptable for regional restraint. Imposing limitations on missile ranges would involve three possible alternatives: banning systems that exceed a set range limit, even if they have already been flight tested or deployed; making exceptions for certain systems and, therefore, freezing in place disparities in arsenals; or allowing all participants to match the range capabilities of the most advanced regional power. In the case of the Middle East, the first two of these alternatives would probably be, in the near term, politically and militarily unacceptable to one or several regional powers, and the third would vitiate the meaning of range limitations entirely.

In any case, the proximity of adversarial states in the Middle East and the Persian Gulf would make it difficult to negotiate range limitations low enough to be militarily meaningful. Range limitations also would be difficult to verify. Missiles can be adapted to longer ranges by adjusting payloads or altering rocket engine efficiency, and although these adaptations may still be technically difficult for some states, restraints on conversion efforts would be difficult to enforce. It is inherently difficult to monitor the activities of short-range missile forces deployed on mobile launchers.[22]

Unlike combat aircraft, which rely on fixed air bases typically consisting of long runways, multiple taxiways, hardened aircraft shelters, fortified repair and supply facilities, and underground command posts, a ballistic missile force can be little more than a handful of mobile launchers and support vehicles. Crews do not need to fire actual missiles in order to train and, as a result, operational capabilities can be maintained even in the absence of visible equipment tests.[23] Whereas an air force requires years to be created, a missile force can be trained and equipped in months if provided with equipment by an external supplier.[24]

Despite these obstacles, the elimination of certain classes of missiles—if this act were to lead to the eventual elimination of all missile forces in the region—would be a positive step toward enhanced stability in the Middle East. Although many definitional problems arise in considering which systems would be covered, how to devise requisite enforcement and compliance measures, and which countries to include, it is indisputable that a regionwide ban on missiles would be far easier to manage than a selective effort to constrain technical characteristics and sizes of missile arsenals.

Confidence- and Security-Building Measures

These considerations suggest that the pursuit of a missile restraint regime in the Middle East should focus initially on building confidence among the countries of the region concerning missiles. Confidence- and security-building measures (CSBMs)—including information and intelligence exchanges, on-site inspections (OSIs) of defense production and space launch facilities, prior notification of missile tests, and other mechanisms that promote consultation among regional rivals—could help ease unwarranted suspicions about missile production efforts, limit their political and military consequences, and, possibly, reduce some of the incentives now propelling the expansion of these programs.

CSBMs regarding missiles could help reduce tensions by mitigating the mystery about rivals' military activities, providing channels for routine interaction, and demonstrating adversaries' interest in reassuring other states about their military objectives. Although these instruments are only valuable as indicators of political will and can be violated at any time, they can help establish the kind of diplomatic infrastructure that ultimately would be needed for broader accommodation. Declarations of intent, such as pledges not to use ballistic missiles preemptively, would probably not endure in a crisis, but they would nevertheless serve as indicators of political conciliation, which should not be dismissed out of hand. Similarly, OSIs and prior notification of test launches do nothing to stop dedicated missile programs, but they might help reduce the climate of suspicion among adversaries through increased communication.

The United States has explored these kinds of initiatives with Middle East partners over the past few years. In late 1988, for example, the United States reportedly held discussions with both Egypt and Israel concerning missile-related CBMs. According to press reports, among the proposals mentioned were notifications of missile launches, whether planned missile tests or practice firings of operational systems. Some U.S. government officials also advocated that countries in the region adopt a "no first use" policy toward missiles.[25]

More ambitious CSBMs have been proposed by private analysts, including Thomas Hirschfeld, an authority on CBMs in Europe. He has usefully suggested a basket of initiatives regarding missiles that should be considered in the Middle East, including the following:

- Prohibition of concealment to overhead observation.
- Advance notification of the date, launch area, and planned impact point of missile firing tests.
- In the event of hostilities, or preparation for hostilities, third parties could establish channels for communicating continued intentions not to use ballistic missiles and, in particular, not to use loads like gas or nuclear weapons.[26]

It is clear that missile-related CBMs already play a role in the region. Following Saudi Arabia's acquisition of intermediate-range DF-3A missiles in 1988, the United States and Egypt attempted to minimize Israel's negative response to the delivery. At the same time, an effort was made to reassure the Saudis concerning possible Israeli reactions. Saudi Arabia agreed to adhere to the Nuclear Non-Proliferation Treaty (NPT). In addition, Saudi Arabia indicated that it had no intention to use the missiles preemptively against Israel, and the Israelis responded by denying any plans to launch preventive attacks on the missiles. These communications appear to have significantly reduced tensions resulting from the missiles' arrival in the region.

Other CSBMs that could be considered for missile restraint include the application of international safeguards and on-site verification at space launch facilities to ensure they are not being used to develop missiles; the development of an international space launch agency to give countries access to space in return for not producing their own space launch vehicles; regional export controls, such as agreements among the countries of the region not to sell missiles to unstable states; and routine bilateral military exchanges between rival states to discuss common security concerns.

Subsequent efforts regarding agreements to delimit missile deployment areas—moving forces away from borders, for instance, and declaring fixed deployment sites that could be subject to monitoring—could reduce the threat or perceived threat of surprise attack and, in principle, be stabilizing measures. Such deployment limitations should be thought of as a potentially important element of a more comprehensive regional or bilateral security pact among the region's nations. The Sinai agreement, which provides for peacekeeping forces and other enforcement mechanisms to monitor proscribed military activities in the area, already represents a historic achievement in the region and has helped enhance stability and mitigate tensions between Israel and Egypt since 1974.[27]

Conclusion

Although achieving significant curbs on the demand for missiles will depend on progress in reducing overall regional tensions in the Middle East, this broader objective can be helped by encouraging states to pursue incremental measures aimed at enhancing confidence among the nations of the region. The United States can play an important role in encouraging regional powers to pursue CSBMs, although the suitability of initiatives must ultimately be judged by the states themselves and must reflect local realities.

As a first step, the United States should take the lead in helping countries develop routine consultative mechanisms for exchanging information about military programs, discussions of mutual security concerns, and, over time, consideration of more ambitious arms control measures. The United States is a source of leadership and operational expertise about such mechanisms, which Third World countries are often genuinely unfamiliar with. Indeed, even U.S. assistance in such prosaic areas as customs enforcement, automated data collection for assessing force balances, or mechanisms to monitor exports is useful. Such assistance was apparently decisive in enabling the Chinese government to place tighter controls on its export of missiles, for example.

The effectiveness of U.S. diplomatic efforts will require avoiding an exaggerated political profile, which is almost always the undoing of sensitive diplomacy. Moreover, the United States and its western allies should not bear disproportionate responsibility for encouraging restraint. Other missile suppliers, including China, the former Soviet Union, and Third World arms suppliers, must be induced to cooperate.

In order for ballistic missile arms control agreements to become attractive to countries in the Middle East, such efforts must offer demonstrable benefits that are not attainable through other means. Most countries in this region of the world have limited familiarity with arms control concepts and are suspicious of negotiated security arrangements that require reductions in military capabilities. The means by which countries might be encouraged toward nonaggressive and deterrent postures as they acquire new weapon capabilities are not well understood. The predominant focus of industrial countries' policies for containing regional missile arsenals has been on preventing the technology from proliferating, not on what to do once prevention has failed. In the end, negotiated efforts to restrain missile programs are most likely to be effective if they are pursued following the institutionalization of incremental CBMs and as part of initiatives to end or contain regional conflicts. As such, ballistic missile arms control measures will be but one of several efforts intended to manage the transition to a genuinely interdependent international system that has more codified means of resolving disputes peacefully. This will be the key challenge for the future security of the Middle East.

5. Chemical Weapons Arms Control

Charles Flowerree and Brad Roberts

Negotiated measures to control or eliminate stockpiles of chemical weapons (CW) in the Middle East remain elusive. Several countries in the region have chemical weapons but only Iraq acknowledges possession. All other states deny their existence and have declaratory policies not always consistent with information reported from a wide variety of sources. This circumstance is hardly unique to the region, however. Aside from Iraq, only the United States and the former Soviet Union admit to possessing chemical weapons, although twenty or more countries may possess such weapons or actively seek their possession.

This point of epistemology has important implications for arms control in the Middle East. Because discussion of chemical weapons, analysis of their implications, and speculation about reasonable policy alternatives occur under a shadow of inadequate information, the debate within the region about chemical weapons can be very stilted. It is often difficult to discern the real thinking of key decision makers about the purposes of their chemical weapons programs, the significance they attach to retention of specific military capabilities, or the possible benefits of negotiated measures.

In a region not renowned for its ability to discuss either peace or arms control, it is not surprising that the subject of chemical weapons arms control has received high doses of rhetoric but scant serious attention. The interesting question is whether the accumulation of weapons of all kinds in the region, and the specter of a type of war in the region heretofore unknown—a war with unacceptable consequences for all parties—has changed or will change attitudes in the region toward chemical weapons arms control.

The Middle East peace process begun October 1991 in Madrid may produce outcomes relevant to regional CW arms control. If it lives up to the ambitions of its most optimistic supporters, the peace process may restructure regional relations on a less militaristic basis so that many new arms control possibilities are created, whether regional or transregional (i.e., involving the region in broader measures). If the process stagnates, it may increase interest in low-cost confidence-building measures (CBMs), of which chemical weapons arms control might be one. If the peace process collapses, the chemical arms control enterprise will falter badly, unless a catastrophic war breaks out— such a war might result in the kind of control now being forced upon Iraq by the United Nations in the wake of its defeat in the Persian Gulf War.

This chapter describes and evaluates CW arms control alternatives. It begins with a review of the chemical warfare capabilities of states in the region and an assessment of their importance for regional stability. It then analyzes the two primary paths to chemical weapons arms control in the Middle East—the global approach embodied in the ongoing negotiations to achieve a comprehensive Chemical Weapons Convention (CWC) and the regional approach. Policy options for states not in the region that want to ameliorate the chemical weapons problem if negotiated measures fail or are slow to develop are also discussed. The chapter concludes with a discussion of future prospects for chemical weapons arms control in the Middle East.

The Status of Regional Capabilities

The most comprehensive statement by a U.S. official regarding the status of chemical weapons programs in the Middle East was made by Admiral Thomas Brooks, director of Naval Intelligence, in testimony to the House Armed Services Committee soon after the Persian Gulf War.[1] Brooks provided a chart with his testimony, which listed the following Middle Eastern countries as probable possessors of chemical weapons: Iraq, Egypt, Iran, Israel, Libya, and Syria. Saudi Arabia was listed as a state that "may possess" chemical weapons. Using publicly available information, the capabilities of these states can be summarily described as follows.[2]

Iraq

Iraq was required to declare the full contents of its chemical weapons stockpile and production capability under the terms of the UN cease-fire that ended the Persian Gulf War and to submit all elements of its chemical weapons capability to destruction. Its original declaration reported possession of about 75 tons of Sarin and 500 tons of Tabun, both nerve agents, 280 tons of mustard gas, and 650 tons of chemical precursors. Munitions reported were 1,481 filled artillery shells and bombs as well as 30 chemical warheads for the Al-Hussein missile. The Iraqis also declared that five chemical weapons facilities and five workshops for filling various munitions with poisonous gases had been destroyed in the war.[3] By autumn 1991, after a number of inspections by the UN Special Commission and subsequent revisions by Iraq to its original declarations, the numbers had grown to 45,000 filled chemical munitions, 600–700 tons of chemical agents in bulk containers, and hundreds of tons of precursors.[4] Doubts remain about even these estimates. According to press reports of a U.S. intelligence assessment, about 60 percent of Iraq's chemical and biological warfare capability was damaged during the war.[5]

Iraq is a party to the Geneva Protocol of 1925 but reserved the right to respond in kind if attacked with chemical weapons. When in 1988 Iraq finally admitted to having used chemical weapons against Iran, it stated that this use was in response to Iranian first use. In December 1990, Saddam Hussein stated that Iraq "has the right to possess the weapons which its enemy has; it is also Iraq's right to possess the weapons which match its enemy's weapons."[6]

Egypt

Egypt is another one of the handful of countries to have used chemical weapons since World War I, having employed them during the civil war in Yemen that lasted from 1963 to 1967.[7] The scale of use was limited and the weapons probably did not come from indigenous production. Egypt's offensive CW capabilities were long understood to be in keeping with its Soviet-supplied or -designed armor and other equipment and the Soviet influence on its military doctrine. But in recent years there have been indications that Egypt has been accumulating the industrial infrastructure for nerve gas production without importing controlled precursor chemicals.

A policy of hedging its bets by creating a chemical capability would be consistent with Egypt's political and geographic situation. After the 1973 war, the U.S. press reported that Egyptian leaders were considering building a nerve gas capability to deter Israeli use of nuclear weapons,[8] and senior Egyptian scientists expressed concern about Israeli planning in this regard at international conferences.[9] Although since the Camp David Accords tensions on the border with Israel have lessened, Egypt continues to be conscious of Israel's probable nuclear and possible CW capabilities, and thus might well have contingency plans should relations deteriorate again. In the wake of press reports of a new Egyptian chemical weapons agent plant in March 1989, a U.S. official reportedly said that acquiring chemical weapons could be considered "prudent defense planning" by Egypt, in the light of growing CW production capabilities in neighboring states.[10] The former head of Egypt's CW organization told a reporter in 1988 that Arabs should acquire chemical and biological weapons as a deterrent against the Israeli nuclear threat until they can develop a matching nuclear deterrent.[11]

Egypt became a party to the Geneva Protocol in 1928, without any formal reservation.[12] In 1988 the Egyptian ambassador to the Conference on Disarmament declared that "Egypt does not produce, develop or stockpile such [chemical] weapons, which it rightly regards as weapons of mass destruction that should be banned."[13] In April 1989, after President Hosni Mubarak's visit to Washington, a senior U.S. administration official is quoted as saying that Mubarak "very emphatically made clear that his government was not, repeat not, involved in the production of chemical weapons."[14]

Iran

Iran's reported interest in chemical warfare—both defensive and offensive—can be traced to the Iraqi attacks it suffered for five years and to Iraq's continued production of mustard and nerve gases after that war ended. The weight of publicly available information tends to confirm Iran's claim, made as early as April 1984, that it has the capability to manufacture chemical munitions and strongly suggests that it may already have done so. The information also suggests, but less strongly, that Iranian forces may have employed CW munitions in the war with Iraq. If such weapons were employed, they could have been indigenously manufactured or acquired from abroad, possibly including recovered Iraqi bombs or shells. Iran's military planning has been affected not only by its relations with Iraq but also by its pretensions as a military power in the Persian Gulf area. Thus, the denuding of Iraq's arsenal may not necessarily lead Iran to eliminate its own chemical weapons.

Iran became a party to the Geneva Protocol in 1929. It made no reservations that would permit it the right to in-kind retaliation.[15] In mid-1984 the Iranian deputy foreign minister said in Teheran that "the Islamic Republic of Iran has not and will not use chemical weapons"[16] and thus implied that Iran would not retaliate in kind against Iraq. But in May 1985 Foreign Minister Ali Akbar Velayati told a meeting of diplomats, "Now, faced with such an aggressor, we would like to ask the international community if there exists for the Islamic Republic of Iran any other option but to retaliate. Or, is there still room to resort to multilateral and international means in order to avoid direct action, unilaterally?"[17]

Israel

Israel has been reported to possess chemical weapons, although even less definitive information is available on its CW capability than on its nuclear one. Although there is little public evidence, most analyses agree that Israel has probably developed and produced chemical munitions, paralleling the development of its nuclear capability. Most of the detailed information in support of this view derives from accusations exchanged by Israel and Syria. Until 1984 Israel was the only noncommunist country openly named in any official U.S. statement as a possessor of CW munitions.

Israel's interest in chemical weapons may date from Egypt's CW attacks in Yemen in the mid-1960s. In the intervening years Israel has progressed through the stage of testing indigenously produced protective equipment and CW munitions and may now be constructing a dedicated facility for the production of CW agents and munitions. Earlier, Israel's stockpiles probably consisted, in the main, of nonlethal warfare chemicals. Given the persistence of the allegations and Israel's geopolitical situation, as well as its industrial capabilities, specific evidence in the public record concerning an offensive CW program is surprisingly weak.

A factor in Israeli thinking regarding the chemical threat may be the fact that four Arab states that are parties to the Geneva Protocol—Libya, Syria, Jordan, and Kuwait—reserved the right to retaliate in kind if chemical weapons were used against them. However, two of these countries that pose a credible threat, Libya and Syria, did not make the common Arab reservation that the Protocol was binding only with regard to other parties. Therefore, publicly, they are bound to a no-first-use policy against any country.

Israel became a party to the Geneva Protocol in 1969, reserving the right of retaliation. Until recently, Israeli spokesmen made no official denial of having an offensive CW capability, while at the same time Israel's protective capability had been officially publicized. As late as 1988, a reporter for the *Los Angeles Times*, who found Israeli officials evasive on the question of production or stockpiling, said, "One high-ranking official admitted that the country produces poison gas to carry out defensive tests." The report went on to quote the official as stating, "Any country with a modest chemical industry can make gas weapons. If we need them we can get them."[18]

But recently several official spokesmen have made emphatic denials. At the January 1989 Paris gathering of Geneva Protocol signatories, Deputy Foreign Minister Binyamin Netanyahu told a British reporter who asked if Israel possessed chemical weapons, "No, we do not."[19] Two months later a Foreign Ministry spokesperson said, "Israel does not manufacture chemical weapons."[20]

Libya

Libya is high on the list of Middle East countries suspected of actively seeking a chemical weapons capability. The discovery of a presumed chemical weapons manufacturing plant at Rabta, whose existence became public in 1988, is the principal basis for this concern. During the civil war in Chad in the 1980s there were allegations that Libyan forces had used chemical weapons against Chadian government troops. However, if true, the chemical agents were not of Libyan manufacture.

Libya had some of the earliest experience with gas warfare— in the late 1920s it suffered mustard gas bombings authorized by Mussolini.[21] Now, relatively isolated from potential ene- mies, Libya's requirement for a well-equipped military estab- lishment derives principally from the policies followed by its erratic leader, Muammar Qaddafi. The professed ultimate goal of Libyan foreign policy is to destroy the Israeli presence in the Middle East. Meddling in the affairs of other states of the region has been characteristic of Libyan policy since Qaddafi came to power in 1969. Under his leadership, Libyan armed forces have been equipped fairly lavishly, principally by the Soviet Union. However, Libyan forces have not shown themselves to be par- ticularly effective in combat, and, unlike the other CW suspect states in the Middle East, Libya has no recognized ability to engage in combat involving an exchange of CW munitions. Its role might possibly be as a supplier of chemical warfare agents to other Arab states, if its production facilities are indeed opera- tional. There were reports during the Iran-Iraq War of Libya's supplying various types of military equipment (not of indige- nous production) to Iran.

For over a year and a half following the first allegations about suspected CW production facilities at Rabta, the official Libyan press repeatedly published forceful denials of any effort or intent to acquire an offensive CW capability, culminating in a November 1988 letter to the UN secretary general.[22]

The day before his address to the Paris conference held in January 1989, the Libyan foreign minister told a French inter- viewer, "Despite the fact that the production of chemical weap- ons is not banned by the Geneva agreement, Libya has decided of her own free will that it will not produce, and furthermore does not intend to produce, chemical weapons."[23]

Following a supposed fire in or near the Rabta chemical plant on March 14, 1990, Qaddafi made a statement, the gist of which was given in a Tripoli radio station broadcast. Referring to weapons of mass destruction, Qaddafi reportedly said:

> If Libya could manufacture them it would not have hesitated, and it would not have hidden that fact, because unfortunately there is no law whatsoever to stop any country from manufacturing them. However, Libya on its own and by its own efforts needs another 20 years to produce a chemical bomb.
>
> I challenge any company or state to come to Libya to build a chemical factory. I would personally sign the contract without hesitation, and I would pay 1 billion [currency not specified] to anyone who could build a chemical factory for Libya, because the world has not yet forbidden that.[24]

Libya became a party to the Geneva Protocol in 1971 (two years after the coup bringing Qaddafi to power and eighteen years after gaining independence from Italy), reserving the right to in-kind retaliation. At that time, Libya made the common Arab reservation that accession does not constitute recognition of, or involve treaty relations with, Israel.

Syria

Syria has been reported to possess chemical weapons since the early 1970s; however, there is reason to doubt the earliest reports. But the greater physical detail in reports of both production and deployment of CW munitions in the latter half of the 1980s makes Syria, after Iraq, the most certain proliferator within the region, ahead of Iran and Israel. Still, current reports focus on the munitions side and are weak on details of chemical infrastructure, protective measures, and training and exercises.

A brief examination of Syria's military situation before the Persian Gulf War suggests that from its viewpoint the development of chemical capabilities might have been seen as prudent. The weakening of Syria's security relationship with the Soviet Union after the 1982 skirmish with Israel, and its subsequent backing of Iran in the Iran-Iraq Gulf War, left Syria isolated and militarily vulnerable. The concurrent rise of a chemical threat from Iraq, in addition to the purported stockpile in Israel since the early 1970s, might have been sufficient to start Syria in pursuit of an offensive, in-kind capability. Previous Soviet CW assistance, which was probably purely defensive, could be seen as an inadequate deterrent by itself. The disclosures by Mordechai Vanunu concerning Israel's nuclear program[25] may have stimulated Syrian interest in military capabilities of significant strategic leverage, and chemical weapons might have been seen as suited to this task.

The Syrian Arab Republic became a party to the Geneva Protocol in 1968 (two months ahead of Israel) and did not reserve the right to in-kind retaliation. Syria has made no declaration on possession of chemical weapons. However, during the January 1989 Paris conference its foreign minister used language that seemed as equivocal as that used by the Iraqis and Soviets before either of them admitted to having chemical weapons: "The minister affirmed that, whether or not it has chemical weapons, Syria believes that scrapping one category of weapons of mass destruction while leaving other categories unscrapped is tantamount to unilateral disarmament. [Foreign Minister] al-Shara' announced that Syria is ready to commit itself to scrapping all weapons of mass destruction if Israel is ready to reciprocate."[26] The second sentence could be read as implying that Syria has chemical munitions, but it also might simply be rhetoric.

Regional Implications

A logical question flows from this description of the military capabilities and declaratory policies of the chemically armed states of the Middle East—so what? Why should we concern ourselves with weapons whose history in the region dates back decades and yet have not been decisive in any of its many conflicts?

The short answer is that the problem posed by chemical weapons in the region has taken on qualitative new dimensions in the 1990s. A longer answer follows.

First, to the extent that the publicly available information makes it possible to assess, it seems likely that the proliferation of chemical weapons in the region rapidly accelerated over the past decade. More states became chemical weapons possessors. States with existing offensive capabilities expanded those capabilities with larger and more diverse arsenals, including especially the more lethal nerve agents. Some states increased their abilities to produce chemical warfare agents and munitions from indigenous sources. Most important, however, was the fielding in the past decade of large numbers of long-range delivery systems—aircraft or missiles—that create military options beyond tactical applications to strategic—that is, counter-city—ones.

Second, the growth of chemical weapons capabilities in the region helped lead to their use. Iraq's employment of chemical weapons in its war against Iran and its periodic use domestically against the Kurdish population, both at Halbja in the 1980s and reportedly during the suppression of the rebellion immediately after Iraq's defeat at the hands of the UN coalition, constitute a significant violation of the international norm against the use of chemical weapons. This norm, embodied in the commitment of most of the states of the world to the Geneva Protocol, has been an important barrier to the proliferation of chemical weapons and has constituted one of the few agreed rules among states of vastly different outlooks. Its transgression by Iraq has reminded the international community of its importance.

Third, the existence of chemical arsenals with the potential to be mated to long-range delivery systems has further encouraged destabilizing military competition in the region. This situation has had the effect of eroding stability in times of crisis because of the fear that states would feel compelled to strike preemptively against long-range capabilities. It has strengthened the perceived ability of regional actors to politically coerce their neighbors or influential powers outside the region. It has raised the possible costs of military intervention by outside states in their roles as guarantors of security. It has placed new instruments in the hands of state sponsors of terrorism. And it has increased the likelihood that any future war would be so indiscriminate in its consequences as to cause massive casualties among the various Arab and Israeli peoples packed so tightly together in the region.

Fourth, proliferation of weapons of mass destruction—chemical, nuclear, and biological—combined with the region-wide concern about Iraq's use and threatened use of chemical weapons for purposes of aggrandizement may have paradoxically created incentives for states to find more peaceful ways to manage their conflicts, as exemplified by the beginning of peace negotiations in Madrid in October 1991. The East-West conflict provides a kind of analogy here—the accretion of ever more robust and sophisticated military capabilities brought the United States and Soviet Union to a place where outright war between them became unthinkable, and under the stalemate wrought by the fear that both had more to lose than gain by war, their relationship was transformed. This is not to argue that all chemical weapons in the Middle East exist solely as a component of the Arab-Israeli strategic equation; indeed, Arab chemical weapons have been used not against Israeli targets but against others. However, throughout the region, the military capabilities of high strategic importance—which might include the chemical arsenals of some of the states—are now linked inextricably to the political context in which future choices of war and peace will be made.

If there is to be a negotiated resolution of the chemical weapons problem in the Middle East, it will be of one of two kinds.

Either chemical arms control and disarmament will proceed as part of a global effort to eliminate chemical weapons, now well advanced in the Geneva-based Conference on Disarmament (CD) negotiations for a comprehensive CWC. Or regional measures—whether to eliminate chemical weapons or simply to control the future development of regional CW capabilities—will be implemented. These two paths are discussed in the following sections.

The Chemical Weapons Convention

Efforts to eliminate chemical weapons began in the 1970s and a multilateral CWC has been under negotiation in Geneva since the early 1980s. The goal of the thirty-nine participant nations at the CD and the thirty-seven observers is a chemical weapons disarmament agreement that is global in scope, comprehensive in its application, and fully verifiable. A good deal of confidence exists in mid-1992 that these negotiations will reach a conclusion before the end of the year. But agreement is by no means certain. In any case, it is an open question whether the chemical weapons states of the Middle East would necessarily accede to a CWC if such an international agreement were concluded in 1992. Nevertheless, each of the Middle Eastern countries of concern to CW arms control has a presence at the negotiations in Geneva, whether as a participant (Egypt and Iran) or as an observer (the so-called nonmember participant states: Iraq, Israel, Libya, and Syria).[27]

It is not appropriate to review here the factors inhibiting or helping the drive toward the successful conclusion of the CWC negotiations.[28] It is useful, however, to note those issues remaining under discussion that both shape and reflect the thinking of countries of the Middle East about the utility of the CWC and chemical weapons arms control to their national interests.

One such issue is the provision of assistance to states suffering the consequences of noncompliance by a hostile neighbor. This issue divides the negotiators in Geneva along North-South lines and, hence, is particularly relevant to the Middle East problem. The current text of the CWC provides for an article on assistance (Article X) on which thus far there has been no agreement. The provisional text notes some categories of assistance that might be provided to the parties. Assistance can consist of providing equipment such as CW alarm systems, protective and decontamination equipment, and antidotes as well as information and advice in any of these areas. It can also encompass the concept of "security assurances"; that is, a commitment to provide military protection to a state when chemical weapons are used against it or when the activities of another state suggest a chemical attack is imminent.

In general, the developed countries are chary of open-ended commitments of this sort. They argue that any commitment should be essentially voluntary and that maximum discretion should be given to states to decide what types and levels of assistance might be appropriate. Many developing countries argue that such assurances are vital to their security after a convention enters into force. In an April 1991 article on this subject, Pakistan's ambassador to the CD, Ahmad Kamal, is quoted as stating, "As long as some countries with a chemical weapons capability remain outside the Convention, those which have given up the option would continue to feel threatened and the prohibition regime would remain incomplete and fragile. It is, therefore, necessary that the Convention should contain mandatory provisions on assistance. . . ."[29]

Provisions for security assurances and assistance in the CWC would be particularly helpful in the context of Middle East chemical weapons control. Such provisions can have a positive effect on the CWC by, inter alia, providing inducements to states to sign on to the convention, inhibiting treaty violations or analogous behavior by nonparties, and reducing the likelihood that a victim state would opt to engage in reciprocal violations or even withdraw from the agreement.

A second issue relates to the role of sanctions in responding to noncompliance. A question having particular relevance to the Middle East is whether and how to include sanctions in the CWC.[30] There is considerable support for incorporating a provision calling for the automatic imposition of strict sanctions against states that violate the convention's provisions.

Many states, however, recognizing the difficulty of coordinating and imposing sanctions by the international community, stress that individual countries can decide, even in the absence of a CWC, to impose sanctions against states that use chemical weapons or attempt to develop them.[31] Several countries, including the United States, have adopted laws or regulations concerning sanctions that would be triggered by the use of chemical weapons or by a country's efforts to obtain a chemical weapons capability.

In the United States a sanctions bill, the Chemical and Biological Weapons Control Bill of 1990, was passed by both houses of Congress but vetoed by President Bush in November 1990. The executive branch's reluctance to agree to the automatic sanctions mandated by the 1990 legislation and again by legislation approved by Congress in 1991 reflected a legitimate concern that situations in which sanctions might be imposed are not always clear-cut. The executive branch always seeks freedom to maneuver, taking into account other political and strategic interests that lie outside the arms control area. As an alternative to the legislated sanctions, the president issued an executive order in November 1990 that would impose many of the same sanctions that were included in the vetoed bill. It set forth stringent export regulations and listed various types of sanctions against foreign persons and governments that "knowingly and materially" contribute to the efforts of another country to acquire the capability to develop, produce, stockpile, deliver, or use chemical or biological weapons.[32] However, the executive order gives the secretary of state authority to decide when sanctions would not be in the best interests of the United States.

The problem with sanctions that are not automatically invoked is that they are taken less seriously by countries that might be affected under the assumption that they can always adduce a reason why they ought not to be imposed in a particular instance. Some experts suggest that a possible approach to the problem of automaticity of sanctions would be to key them to the seriousness and clarity of the violation.[33] Use of chemical weapons, for example, could trigger an automatic response, while shipments of possible CW precursors by private firms could be treated with more leeway, reflecting the lesser level of violation and often greater uncertainty about the facts.

After the West's failure to respond vigorously to Iraq's use of chemicals against Iran, it is especially important that a credible sanctions strategy be established. The United States acting alone in imposing sanctions would not create the necessary presumption that violation of chemical weapons norms would result in punishment for the violator. All the main producer nations will have to coordinate in a sanctions strategy for it to be effective.

A third issue in the CWC negotiations relates to the degree of intrusiveness necessary to establish compliance or noncompliance at undeclared facilities. The states of the erstwhile nonaligned world until recently have been largely silent during the debate within the CD's western group and between that group and the former Soviet Union on the subject of challenge inspections. When in 1990 and 1991 it became increasingly apparent that the United States and the former Soviet Union were indeed seriously committed to the conclusion of the CWC negotiations and the implementation of a global ban, these other, long-silent states began to articulate their concerns. Interviews with participants in the CD process indicate that a major concern among the states outside the highly industrialized world is the very intrusive nature of the challenge inspections proposed in the draft treaty presented in 1984 by then–vice president George Bush. In particular, there appear to be real reservations about the possibility that representatives of long-standing regional competitors might have access to sensitive military facilities under a CWC inspection regime.

Here, too, a compromise appears to be in the offing. In July 1991, a new proposal on challenge inspections was presented in Geneva as a joint working paper of the United States, United Kingdom, Japan, and Australia. The proposal struck a balance between the rights of states to conduct challenge inspections of suspect facilities anywhere and anytime with the rights of the challenged state to protect secrets of a military or commercial nature not relevant to CWC compliance. By narrowly circumscribing the right to "anywhere, anytime" inspections as envisioned in the draft 1984 treaty, the proposal was criticized heavily by many states, especially those whose commitment to the principle of highly intrusive inspections had been strengthened by the necessity of such inspections to fully unveil the breadth of Iraq's chemical, biological, nuclear, and missile capabilities. But it was also recognized, grudgingly by some, as representing a logical point of possible consensus among the industrialized nations and those Middle Eastern nations most sharply opposed to intrusive inspections.

A final issue under dispute relates to the conditions under which the convention will enter into force. Specifically, a minority has advocated the retention of the right of in-kind retaliation to chemical attack until the end of the ten-year destruction period envisaged by the CWC. Until recently the United States led this minority, but in May 1991 President Bush issued a statement that substantially modified the U.S. position. He dropped the U.S. insistence on the right to retaliation in-kind until all chemical weapons had been destroyed in accordance with the terms of the convention, as well as the U.S. proposal that the states that possess chemical weapons could retain a small percentage of the stockpiles of chemical weapons (equivalent to 2 percent of the current U.S. stockpile) until all "chemical weapons-capable states" have joined the convention, even after the ten-year destruction period.

The destruction of Iraq's chemical weapons as mandated by the United Nations may provide an important stimulant to the CWC negotiations. Chemical weapons destruction will be a major challenge to those charged with implementing the convention. It is especially daunting for the United States and even more so for the former Soviet states, especially Russia, which face political constraints on the management of their chemical weapons stockpiles, keen environmental interests, and tight pocketbooks. But there is also a question of how quickly and safely states of the developing world will be able to destroy chemical weapons munitions under the regime. The infrastructure put in place to destroy Iraq's chemical arsenal during 1992 and 1993 may be useful for the region as a whole. There may be opportunities to test the feasibility of alternative methods of destruction. Here the United States is in a position to provide technical assistance and, in fact, has offered to do so, both in Iraq and in the former Soviet Union.

Resolution of these key disputes must account fully for the views of the states of the Middle East or they will find a justification—whether pretext or well reasoned—to not accede to the convention. As one Arab close to the chemical disarmament negotiations has argued, "There is only one obstacle before the prohibition of chemical weapons. That is the penchant of states to attempt to ignore the concerns of others."[34] But taking account of these views has not proven easy. The penchant noted above of the Middle Eastern countries to sit aside from the negotiations has hurt. So too has the failure of those states to commit to becoming signatories to the convention should it be completed. Diplomats involved in the negotiation of complex issues are necessarily ill-disposed to sacrifice strongly held positions to parties that have as yet taken no position on their intention to even adhere to the result.

Of course, there is no guarantee that, even if the convention meets the perceived needs of all the participants and observers from the Middle East on each of these issues, it will be effective in gaining full implementation in the region. Any arms control approach that attempts to single out a specific category of weapons or technology faces the inherent problem of the connection of that military capability to the broader spectrum of military assets and the unequal capabilities that different states contribute to military balances. There is a strong argument that the region will not be able to solve its chemical weapons problem until it also solves its nuclear problem and its missile problem and its general war problem. By this argument, arms control and disarmament must follow from, not precede, a peace process. This view does not exclude the long-term possibility of effective chemical disarmament, and indeed some take it as a real possibility given the expectations for the process begun in Madrid.

But the "strategic connectivity" of chemical weapons in the Middle East to other weapons is significant in the thinking of most states. To be sure, each state of the region appears to have different incentives for acquiring chemical weapons. As argued above, most subscribe to the proposition that Arab countries have the right to counter Israel's presumed nuclear and chemical capabilities, even if they do not admit publicly that they themselves possess chemical weapons. Inter-Arab rivalries also have played a role in the Arab countries' decisions about whether to pursue a chemical weapons capability. In this respect, Middle Eastern countries could be divided into subgroups among those whose political and military interests are focused primarily on the Persian Gulf region, those whose attention is riveted on the Israeli question, those whose interests lie in both directions, and those whose interests are inwardly focused.

Nevertheless, if there is one common thread among the Arab countries of the Middle East, it is hostility to or wariness of Israel. But even in this respect, the states of the region differ. Syria's security concerns, for example, have been divided between Israel and Iraq; presumably, in the wake of the Persian

Gulf War, Syria will be less concerned with the threat from Iraq. Egypt, although apparently engaged in a chemical weapons program as a hedge against future changes in the political climate, is less hostile to Israel than its immediate neighbors. Iran's attention is directed primarily toward Iraq and the Persian Gulf region. Libya is violently anti-Israel in its rhetoric, but it is a peripheral factor in the Middle East power equation.

Overall, though, there is no question that the Arab-Israeli conflict is key to progress toward controlling weapons of mass destruction and their long-range delivery systems within the region. So long as Israel feels threatened by Arab territorial and manpower superiority, it will be compelled to compensate by maintaining a technological edge in weaponry. For their part, the Arabs have attempted to link their assertion of the right to possess chemical weapons capabilities to Israel's presumed nuclear capability. As a recent UN study put it, "The close relationship—the linkage—among all the elements that affect security is well known. Nuclear capabilities are linked to chemical weapons, chemical weapons to conventional arms, conventional arms to political conflict. And all these threads are woven into a seamless fabric of fear and insecurity."[35]

However, the CWC, if it is concluded, will likely penetrate into the Middle East even if there are no controls on other types of weapons in the region. In reality, the argument about strategic connectivity has not commanded widespread diplomatic support. Eduard Shevardnadze, during his first stint as Soviet foreign minister, often criticized the approach as an excuse to do nothing about controlling arms in the region. Others see the argument as self-serving for the Arab world and hypocritical, given the use of chemical weapons by Arab states against their own citizens and against one another.

Some states of the Middle East may decide that adherence to the CWC is more in their interest than remaining outside the convention. Conceivably, all states might so decide even if there is no progress on the Arab-Israeli front. The key issues beyond those directly associated with the CWC as discussed above are likely to include the following.

First, states will have to evaluate the actual utility of chemical weapons in their arsenals. Iraq's decision not to use chemical weapons in the Persian Gulf War, or its inability to do so, illustrate what the states of Europe, the United States, and the former Soviet Union have long known—the military benefits of chemical weapons are important but limited, and they are often difficult to realize. Against well-protected forces, chemical weapons have little effect. Against cities protected with sophisticated air defenses (and, in the future, possibly missile defenses), chemical munitions offer uncertain advantages, especially if the population has been prepared with gas masks and an education program. Moreover, retention of a chemical stockpile has downsides of its own. Chemical munitions are difficult to keep serviceable for long periods (witness the dilapidated state of Iraq's arsenal, most of which was produced in just the past few years). If stockpiled in large numbers, these weapons can be counterproductive in military terms—witness the way in which Iraq's chemical capability strengthened the resolve of the anti-Saddam coalition to seek a prompt and decisive military outcome, rather than deterring it from coalescing and going to war.

Second, states will have to evaluate whether possible opponents have the means to negate decisively any possible military advantages of chemical weapons use. Effective protective measures, whether of military forces or civilian populations, are important in this regard. So too are the possession of other military capabilities, such as nuclear or biological weapons and long-range missiles, and especially those that give the state attacked with chemical weapons the possibility of escalating the conflict.

Third, states will have to assess the continued utility of the military option generally. War will not soon pass from the scene in the Middle East. On the other hand, what historian of recent vintage would have expected the great diminution of the threat of nuclear war in Europe or so rapid an end to the Cold War? These monumental changes suggest the possibility that some or all of the states in the region may decide that they are better served by joining the convention than remaining outside it. But of course, this is the optimistic case. Again, Israel will be the key. Even if the CWC negotiations succeed in producing a multilateral treaty to which a large majority of the countries of the world are willing to subscribe, many Arab nations might not adhere unless Israel does so too. As the UN study on a Middle East Nuclear-Weapon-Free Zone summarily noted,

> In specific terms, Israel's neighbors must gain confidence that Israel has no intention of using its superior technical skill, including nuclear technology, to expand its frontiers or to impose an unacceptable settlement of the problem of the Palestinians. Israeli opinion must gain confidence that its neighbors have no intention of using their superior manpower, wealth or other resources to destroy Israel or to impose an unacceptable solution to the problem of the Palestinians.[36]

Regional Approaches

If no international CWC comes about in the near term, what are the alternatives? Are there regional chemical weapons arms control approaches that offer some promise? Theoretically, a number of options exist. Each offers benefits and drawbacks. None offers a certain result.

One principal option is the "big bite" approach—the establishment of a regional zone free of chemical weapons as part of a more comprehensive effort that strips all so-called weapons of mass destruction from the region. Egyptian President Mubarak and former Soviet Foreign Minister Shevardnadze have proposed parallel big bite initiatives.[37] The Soviet proposal was tabled in December 1990 as a possible follow-up action if Iraq were to voluntarily withdraw from Kuwait. Under these circumstances, Shevardnadze said, "What we will have on our agenda as a next item would be a transition of the Middle East" into a region "free of nuclear and chemical weapons."[38]

But ridding the Middle East of weapons of mass destruction in one fell swoop is highly problematic under existing circumstances. Even if all the crucial countries were to agree to the concept, practical problems would arise with respect to the different weapons.

In the biological weapons area, for example, a multilateral treaty already exists—the Biological Weapons Convention of 1972—but its ability to deter or detect violations by treaty signatories or to compel compliance is inadequate.[39] Among the Middle Eastern states, only Iran, Jordan, Kuwait, Lebanon, Qatar, Saudi Arabia, and, following the Persian Gulf War, Iraq have acceded to this convention. As former CIA Director William Webster repeatedly told the Congress in 1990–91, substantial doubts exist about the level of compliance with the Biological Weapons Convention by states in the Middle East.[40]

Further, chemical weapons present a particular problem because both the weapons and the facilities for manufacturing them exist in several countries in the region. This fact means that any zone free of chemical weapons must provide the means of accounting for and destroying existing weapons, dismantling production facilities, and ensuring that critical materials for making chemical weapons agents do not enter the zone, or if they do, are used only for peaceful purposes. In the absence of a CWC, there would be no established verification procedures and appropriate mechanisms to ensure compliance within the zone.

The situation with respect to verification of nuclear weapons is somewhat better since a mechanism exists under the International Atomic Energy Agency (IAEA). But, as the UN study on a nuclear weapons-free zone in the Middle East notes, procedures for expanding and reinforcing present safeguards may be needed. In fact, as UN investigations in Iraq have demonstrated, it will be necessary to develop IAEA procedures that go beyond those currently existing, including maintaining a staff dedicated to handling compliance questions that may arise concerning the zone.

Ensuring that all these requirements are met is a tall order. Moreover, because at this time there are no universal legal strictures against possession and manufacture of chemical weapons and the Nuclear Non-Proliferation Treaty is not universally accepted, countries in the zone would find it virtually impossible to accept the restrictions that a zone would impose while countries elsewhere are not so restrained. A Middle East free of all weapons of mass destruction is a goal that must await less sweeping measures of arms control.

A somewhat more hopeful approach to eliminating chemical and other weapons of mass destruction from the area would be to emphasize initially moving toward a nuclear weapons-free zone while working for early completion of the CWC. At the same time CBMs would be pursued, with the eventual objective of inducing all states in the region to adhere to the international agreements governing weapons of mass destruction.

Progress toward creating a nuclear weapons-free zone in the Middle East would certainly make the elimination or control of other weapons of mass destruction in the area easier to attain. A ray of hope in this regard is the recent statement by Israel's representative to the Amendment Conference of the Parties to the Limited Test Ban Treaty. He said, in part,

> While we view the attainment of a CTB (Comprehensive Test Ban) as an important global objective, we view the establishment of a Nuclear Weapons Free Zone in the Middle East as an imperative regional objective. Only such a zone, freely and directly negotiated by the states concerned, can ensure the non-introduction of nuclear weapons into our region.... Revelations of recent months regarding Iraqi nuclear ambitions have reinforced the judgment that no other legal framework can substitute effectively for a Nuclear Weapons Free Zone.[41]

If such a zone were to come into place, it would inevitably have to be accompanied by agreements on other weapons of mass destruction. The key question is whether measures for chemical weapons arms control, short of comprehensive disarmament, might be envisioned. In short, are there interim, limited arms control measures that might be useful? In fact, it is possible to envision several near-term measures that could dampen the drive toward chemical weapons. The Persian Gulf War may have compelled militarily significant Middle Eastern countries to begin to rethink the proposition that a buildup of mass destruction weapons (which often evokes offsetting responses by their neighbors) does in fact contribute to their security. In particular, chemical weapons may have lost some of their luster as the "poor man's atom bomb." Although not all will agree with this view, the war gave it a new standing that should be encouraged. Western countries might assert the point informally that a primary lesson of that war was that against a technologically advanced military power (Israel as well as Western countries) chemical weapons are unlikely either to deter or to make a significant difference in the outcome. In these circumstances, the possibility arises that one or more countries in the region might take the initiative in considering measures that could lead to the development of a consensus among Arab states that chemical weapons diminish rather than contribute to the security of all. In this regard, the Arab League might establish a subgroup, possibly under Egyptian leadership, to examine attitudes toward chemical weapons and to make recommendations to the member nations. Egypt might wish to use the Arab League forum to build support for Mubarak's plan.

Another type of political CBM that might be feasible would be a pledge by all countries in the area, including Israel, to become original parties to the CWC once it is opened for signature. Several countries have already made such a declaration, in part to nudge the countries that might be holding back.

Another CBM that could contribute to chemical weapons control would be to adopt measures that promote transparency in the military activities of states in the Middle East analogous to the measures that have been adopted in Europe, beginning with the 1975 Final Act of the Conference on Security and Cooperation in Europe. The concept of transparency has since been expanded from the simple process of notification and observation of military exercises to exchanges of data, open skies aerial monitoring, on-site inspections under agreed conditions, establishment of hot lines, and other measures designed to remove the shroud of uncertainty from the military activities of countries in areas of high tension. One noted scholar has argued that some of these measures could be applied in the Middle East to benefit both the peace process and arms control.[42] He suggests the establishment of a Conflict Prevention Center under UN auspices to develop appropriate transparency measures and to oversee their implementation. Whether such an arrangement can be agreed to under present circumstances is open to doubt, but its potential benefits to the achievement of stability and the limitation of armaments, including chemical weapons, warrants a vigorous effort to seek ways to increase transparency in the Middle East.

A transparency measure that might be pursued in conjunction with a diplomatic commitment to become original signatories of the CWC would be for states in the Middle East to make formal declarations of their military capabilities generally or their chemical warfare capabilities in particular. The U.S.-Soviet agreement to exchange data on chemical weapons facilities and stockpiles as a means of facilitating bilateral negotiations and working toward solutions of issues in the CWC negotiations established a useful precedent. Peacemaking in the Middle East might be well served by a similar commitment. It would also be relatively low cost, militarily and politically.

More formal negotiated measures short of comprehensive disarmament are also conceivable. Agreed ceilings on existing CW force levels or production capabilities might be envisioned. Caps on delivery systems, especially long-range ones, could narrowly circumscribe the utility some states might attribute to chemical weapons.[43] The June 1990 bilateral agreement of the United States and the Soviet Union might be a useful model. That agreement committed the two states to destroy the majority (but not all) of their chemical weapons and to cooperate in the task. It provided for verification measures, limited to inspecting declared stockpiles and monitoring the destruction process. It also reflected a prior commitment to halt chemical weapons production.

Whether or not states of the Middle East will find any of these measures useful in the absence of progress on the larger regional peace agenda will be a function of the importance they attach to interim CBMs. There is promise in each step. Each offers a more easily attainable goal than comprehensive chemical disarmament at costs lower than such disarmament. Whether those benefits and costs are seen as important will depend on the commitment of states in the region to peace within the region. Each measure would help build confidence, but the resolution of the political tensions in the region will require actions on all fronts—political, economic, and military.

Control Measures for States Outside the Region

The international community is not devoid of options of its own to deal in some limited fashion with the existence of chemical weapons in the Middle East if nothing results from regional or multilateral arms control efforts. Arrangements for controlling or prohibiting the transfer of the wherewithal to produce chemical weapons already exist. The primary emphasis since the mid-1980s has been the coordination of export controls among the states of the Organization for Economic Cooperation and Development. The Australia Group, an informal group of twenty industrialized nations plus the European Community represented as such, has been instrumental in getting wide agreement on a list of chemical precursors that will come under export controls imposed by the countries belonging to the group. In an agreement reached in Paris on May 30, 1991, Australia Group members committed themselves to adopt controls as stringent as those already in effect in the United States by the end of the year. Companies will be required to obtain licenses before exporting any of the fifty chemicals on the group's list to countries other than those that signed the agreement.[44]

One limiting factor bearing on the effectiveness of the Australia Group is the lack of serious and sustained participation by Middle Eastern countries. With regard to chemical weapons, some countries in the Middle East now can be classified as "industrialized" in that they are able to produce many of the materials required to achieve a chemical weapons capability and some—Libya and Iraq, for instance—have been suspected of developing the ability to export some of these materials. The Australia Group needs to explore the possibilities of building cooperative activities with a number of the countries of the Middle East.

Australia itself is well positioned to lead in this regard. In addition to its active role in the group that bears its name, Australia has the experience of conducting a chemical weapons initiative in the Pacific region and of organizing the Canberra Government-Industry Conference against Chemical Weapons of September 1989. Moreover, it does not have a strongly partisan image with respect to the quarrels of the Middle East. Perhaps by working through the more moderate Arab states, Australia could help develop a common approach to the control of traffic in chemical weapons precursors.

The limited effectiveness of an export-control strategy must be recognized, however. The barriers to chemical armaments today are primarily political, not technical. Many nations have at their disposal the means to make chemical weapons and have turned to overseas suppliers primarily to use the most advanced technology and readily available chemicals. But they need not do so. To the extent nonproliferation efforts suggest a permanent division between countries of the "North" possessing chemical weapons and those of the "South" to whom the "North" would like to deny such weapons, the political consensus underlying the opposition to chemical weapons will evaporate and may actually stimulate proliferation. Moreover, nonproliferation measures must be seen as already having largely failed in the Middle East, where large quantities of chemical munitions and the facilities to produce them appear to exist despite concerted efforts in recent years. Continued efforts could be useful, however, in constraining the expansion of chemical weapons capabilities.

An alternative approach is to emphasize sanctions against those who use chemical weapons. A credible sanctions policy is an important complement to other measures designed to arrest the spread of chemical weapons. Just the threat of sanctions could affect the policy decisions of Middle Eastern countries that may be contemplating embarking on a chemical weapons program. Although sanctions might not stop a determined proliferator, they would add to the costs, both financial and political, for carrying out such a program.

Sanctions have often been disparaged as having failed to accomplish their objectives, with critics citing as an example the failure of the economic and military assistance sanctions aimed at stopping the Pakistan nuclear weapons program. Nevertheless, if the objectives are realistic and the circumstances propitious, sanctions can be effective. Lewis Dunn, a former senior official with the U.S. Arms Control and Disarmament Agency, has noted that the U.S. threat to terminate economic and military assistance to South Korea in the mid-1970s was critical in convincing the South Koreans to give up what could have become a major nuclear weapons program.[45] It is useful to note that sanctions against Iraq are already in existence and the ban on the export to Iraq of materials that can be used for producing chemical weapons should remain until an effective CW arms control regime can be established.

Conclusion

The prospect for the elimination of chemical weapons from the Middle East in the foreseeable future is not bright, but it is not as gloomy as many might think. A variety of measures are quite conceivable and become more possible as the peace negotiating process begun in Madrid in October 1991 unfolds. A global approach may work over time; so too might regional ones.

If efforts to control chemical armaments in the Middle East fail, it is, of course, possible that recognition of the dangers of the continued accumulation of chemical weapons and other weapons of mass destruction might cause the perceptions of political leaders to change and motivate them to take measures to eliminate those weapons through mutual agreement. However, it equally possible that a conflict will erupt while these weapons are still in the hands of antagonistic nations. A cease-fire regime at the end of the fighting might bring about the elimination of such weapons from the arsenals of the combatants, as is being done in Iraq, but at enormous human and economic cost. These considerations argue for continuing to press ahead with the arms control measures discussed here no matter how bleak the prospects for success may be at the moment. And the United States and its allies have a particular responsibility to do everything possible to help solve the political problems that bedevil the Middle East. But chemical weapons arms control efforts need not wait for the achievement of a political settlement in the region. Both need to be pursued with vigor and persistence now.

Notes

1. Platt, "Introduction"

1. "An Interim Report of the United States Institute of Peace's Study Group on Regional Arms Control Arrangements and Issues in the Post-War Middle East" (Washington, D.C.: United States Institute of Peace, 1991), 4.

2. Richard Darilek, "The Future of Conventional Arms Control in Europe: A Tale of Two Cities: Stockholm, Vienna," *Survival* XXIV, no. 1 (January/February 1987):5–16.

3. This classic definition of CSBMs is drawn from Johan Jorgen Holst, "Confidence-Building Measures: A Conceptual Framework," *Survival* XXV, no. 1 (January/February 1983):2.

2. Darilek and Kemp, "Prospects for CSBMs"

1. Volker Kunzendorff, "Verification in Conventional Arms Control," Adelphi Paper no. 245 (London: International Institute for Strategic Studies, Winter 1989), 14–15.

2. John Borawski, *From the Atlantic to the Urals: Negotiating Arms Control at the Stockholm Conference* (Washington, D.C.: Pergamon-Brassey's, 1988), 4–5.

3. This discussion borrows from James E. Goodby, "Transparency in the Middle East," *Arms Control Today* XXI, no. 4 (May 1991):8–9; and Itshak Lederman, "The Arab-Israeli Experience in Verification and Its Relevance to Conventional Arms Control in Europe," Occasional Paper 2 (College Park, Md.: Center for International Security Studies, University of Maryland, 1989). Also, see Michael Krepon and Peter Constable's chapter on "The Role of Aerial Inspections in Confidence Building and Peacemaking" in this volume and Brian Mandell, *The Sinai Experience: Lessons in Multimethod Arms Control Verification and Risk Management*, Arms Control Verification Studies no. 3 (Ottawa:

Arms Control and Disarmament Division, Department of External Affairs, 1987).

4. It is not clear that either the United States or the former Soviet Union harbored any real hopes for arms control "results" from the MBFR talks. The United States wanted to avoid unilateral withdrawals of U.S. troops from western Europe, which then Senate majority leader Mike Mansfield (D.-Mont.) was proposing at the time; the Soviets wanted the CSCE for political and economic reasons. Holding MBFR negotiations was the price for both.

5. Johan Jorgen Holst and Karen Melander, "European Security and Confidence Building Measures," in *Arms Control and Military Force,* ed. Christoph Bertram (London: International Institute for Strategic Studies, 1980), 223–231.

6. Borawski, *From the Atlantic to the Urals,* 29, 58–59.

7. U.S. Arms Control and Disarmament Agency, *Arms Control and Disarmament Agreements* (Washington, D.C., 1987), 326–334.

8. James E. Goodby, *Risk Reduction: A Second Track for Arms Control* (Washington, D.C.: American Association for the Advancement of Science, 1987), 1–13.

9. For an analysis of the CSBMs in the Stockholm Document, see Darilek, "The Future of Conventional Arms Control in Europe," 5–19. This analysis also appears in Chapter 10 of the *Stockholm International Peace Research Institute (SIPRI) Yearbook 1987: World Armaments and Disarmament* (New York: Oxford University Press, 1987), 339–354.

10. For further analyses of various CSBM proposals launched at the Stockholm talks, see Yoav Ben-Horin et al., "Building Confidence and Security in Europe: The Potential Role of Confidence- and Security-Building Measures," R-3431-USDP (Santa Monica, Calif.: The RAND Corporation, December 1986); and James Kahan et al., *Testing the Effects of Confidence- and Security-Building Measures in a Crisis,* R-3517-USDP (Santa Monica, Calif.: The RAND Corporation, December 1987).

11. For NATO's original proposal, see "Text of NATO Proposals for Measures of Information Exchange, Stabilization, Verification, and Non-Circumvention," in *BASIC Reports from Vienna* (Washington, D.C.: British-American Security Information Council, September 21, 1989), 3–7.

12. *Wall Street Journal,* September 22, 1989, p. 10. See also the noncircumvention provision in section V, "Text of NATO Proposals," 7.

13. *Wall Street Journal,* September 22, 1989, p. 10.

14. See *The Vienna Document 1990 of the Negotiations on Confidence-and Security-Building Measures Convened in Accordance with the Relevant Provisions of the Concluding Document of the Vienna Meeting of the Conference on Security and Cooperation in Europe,* which was approved at the CSCE Summit meeting in Paris on November 21, 1990.

15. See Lederman, "The Arab-Israeli Experience."

16. For more details, see Geoffrey Kemp, *The Conduct of the Middle East Arms Race* (Washington, D.C.: Carnegie Endowment for International Peace, 1991), 151–175.

17. Helena Cobban, *The Superpowers and the Syrian-Israeli Conflict,* The Washington Papers (Washington, D.C.: Center for Strategic and International Studies, 1991), 74.

18. Harvey Morris, "Explosion that Led to Ill-fated Mission," *The Independent,* March 16, 1990.

19. See Avner Cohen and Marvin Miller, "Defusing the Nuclear Middle East," *New York Times,* May 30, 1991; and "Establishment of a Nuclear-Weapon-Free Zone in the Region of the Middle East," UN General Assembly, 45th session, agenda item 49, October 10, 1990. Although greater transparency in Israel's nuclear weapons program is demanded by a number of nations in the international community, there are strong countervailing, nonproliferation arguments for keeping Israel's bomb "in the basement" and not disclosing too much information about its capabilities.

20. See Moshe Ma'oz, *Assad: The Sphinx of Damascus* (New York: Weidenfeld and Nicolson, 1988), 138; and Avner Yaniv, *Dilemmas of Security: Politics, Strategy and the Israeli Experience in Lebanon* (New York: Oxford University Press, 1987), 60–61.

21. William Quandt, *Saudi Arabia in the 1980s: Foreign Policy, Security and Oil* (Washington, D.C.: Brookings Institution, 1981), 61.

22. Goodby, "Transparency in the Middle East," 10–11.

23. Thomas J. Hirschfeld, "Mutual Security Short of Arms Control," in *Arms Control in the Middle East,* ed. Dore Gold (Boulder, Colo.: Westview Press, 1991), 34.

24. Ibid., 34–36.

25. Ibid., 36.

26. Goodby, "Transparency in the Middle East," 11.

3. Krepon and Constable, "Role of Aerial Inspections"

1. Johan Jorgen Holst, "Confidence-Building Measures: A Conceptual Framework," *Survival* XXV, no. 1 (January/February 1983):2.

2. The use of aerial inspections within Iraq constitute an entirely separate case of unilateral measures carried out under resolutions adopted by the Security Council directed against a state constituting a threat to the entire region that had waged an aggressive war against a neighbor. Although these aerial operations appear to be quite useful in carrying out the mandate of the UN Special Commission, they do not fall under the scope of this essay.

3. See Amy Smithson, "Multilateral Aerial Inspections," in *Open Skies*, ed. Michael Krepon and Amy Smithson (New York: St. Martin's Press, forthcoming).

4. In this essay, the term "third party" reflects the activities of a single country or a group of countries acting collectively as part of a multinational organization.

5. See Lederman, "The Arab-Israeli Experience"; "An Evaluation of the U.S. Early Warning System in the Sinai," Comptroller General Report to Congress, ID-77-11, June 6, 1977; and "Sinai Agreement," Hearing Before the Committee on Foreign Relations, U.S. Senate, 97th Congress, on S.J. Res. 100, July 20, 1981.

6. For more on the MFO, see "The Multinational Force and Observers: Servants of Peace" (Rome: MFO Office of Public Affairs, November 1990); and U.S. Sinai Field Mission, "Peace in the Sinai" (Washington, D.C.: Department of State, 1982).

7. See Henry Kissinger, *Years of Upheaval* (Boston: Little, Brown and Company, 1982), 1254; and the testimony of Ambassador Michael Sterner, "Sinai Agreement," Hearing Before the Committee on Foreign Relations, U.S. Senate, 97th Congress, on S.J. Res. 100, July 20, 1981, 10.

8. See, for example, Robert B. Houghton and Frank G. Trinka, *Multinational Peacekeeping in the Middle East* (Washington, D.C.: U.S. Department of State, Foreign Service Institute, 1984), 84–88; Paul F. Diehl, "Peacekeeping Operations in the Quest for Peace," *Political Science Quarterly* 103, no. 3 (1988):489–504; Michael Krepon and Jeffrey P. Tracey, " 'Open Skies' and UN Peace-keeping," *Survival* XXXII, no. 3 (May/June 1990):252–253; and "Overhead Remote Sensing for United Nations Peacekeeping," *External Affairs and International Trade, Canada* (April 1990):3–7.

9. Lebanon poses an exception in this regard; its political leaders have not had sufficient national authority for much of the period in which the overflights have been carried out in the Middle East. Political consent also does not bar overflights conducted unilaterally by interested parties, but these practices are beyond the scope of this essay.

10. Richard N. Haass defines the prerequisites of "ripeness" as a shared perception of the desirability of an accord, an ability to agree to one, an ability to compromise in order to reach agreement, and the existence of a mutually acceptable approach or process. *Conflicts Unending, The United States and Regional Disputes* (New Haven, Conn.: Yale University Press, 1990), 27–29.

11. The aircraft in this case was not on an aerial inspection flight. See "The Blue Helmets: A Review of United Nations Peace-keeping" (New York: UN Department of Public Information, August 1990), 109; John Mackinlay, *The Peacekeepers: An Assessment of Peacekeeping Operations at the Arab-Israeli Interface* (London: Unwin Hyman, 1989), 143; and Fred Gaffen, *The Eye of the Storm: A History of Canadian Peacekeeping* (Toronto: Deneau and Wayne, 1987), 133.

12. "An Evaluation of the U.S. Early Warning System in the Sinai" (Washington, D.C.: U.S. General Accounting Office, June 6, 1977), 59.

13. The authors are unaware of any nighttime aerial inspection missions that have been flown in the Middle East and suspect that these may be difficult to negotiate. For a discussion of sensors, see "Overhead Remote Sensing for United Nations Peacekeeping," 8–32; Allen Banner, "Open Skies: Sensors and Platforms," in *Open Skies: Technical, Organizational, Operational, Legal, and Political Aspects*, ed. Michael Slack and Heather Chestnutt (Toronto: Center for International and Strategic Studies, York University, 1990), 3–21; and Krepon and Tracey, " 'Open Skies' and UN Peace-keeping," 255–258.

14. The necessity for established ground rules and sound logistical and financial support for third-party aerial operations was never more apparent than in the UN Yemen Observer Mission in 1963 and 1964. See Major General Carl von Horn, *Soldiering for Peace* (New York: David McKay Company, 1967), 334–356.

15. See the U.S. Sinai Support Mission, "Watch in the Sinai," Department of State publication no. 9131, General Foreign Policy ser. 321 (Washington, D.C.: June 1980), 16.

16. U.S. Sinai Field Mission, "Peace in the Sinai" (Washington, D.C.: Department of State, 1982), 9.

17. "The Blue Helmets," 82, 423.

18. "Peace in the Sinai," 9.

19. See Mandell, *The Sinai Experience,* 13; and David Barton, "The Sinai Peacekeeping Experience: A Verification Paradigm for Europe," *SIPRI Yearbook, 1985* (London: Taylor and Francis, 1985), 543, 549. Arguably, participating states may have accepted these ground rules on the basis that the United States already had the means to carry out aircraft and satellite surveillance of the region, as well as established patterns of intelligence cooperation. As such, agreed overflights by the United States simply reflected the status quo, except to add a new requirement for symmetrical distribution of data or summary information derived from the overflights to the participating states. The Open Skies and CFE negotiations have been far more complicated, in that many countries with quite disparate sensor and processing capabilities would carry out overflights.

20. See "Existing Practices" earlier in this chapter.

21. Much useful work has been done in monitoring heat emissions from nuclear facilities by Intera Technologies, Ltd. See "Airborne Remote Sensing for Multilateral Verification," briefing presented to the Multilateral Verification Project of the Henry L. Stimson Center, November 1989.

22. See Report of the Secretary General, "Establishment of a Nuclear-Weapon-Free Zone in the Region of the Middle East," A/45/435, October 10, 1990, 31–35.

4. Carus and Nolan, "Proliferation of Ballistic Missiles"

1. Ballistic missile forces in the Middle East have been the subject of extensive analysis. Articles include Mark A. Heller, "Coping with Missile Proliferation in the Middle East," *Orbis* (Winter 1991):15–28; and Martin S. Navias, "Ballistic Missile Proliferation in the Middle East," *Survival* (May/June 1989):225–239. Two additional studies that examine missile proliferation country by country are Aaron Karp, "Ballistic Missile Proliferation in the Third World," *SIPRI Yearbook 1989* (New York: Oxford University Press, 1989), 287–318; and Robert D. Shuey and others, "Missile Proliferation: Survey of Emerging Missile Forces," 88-642F (Washington, D.C.: Congressional Research Service, October 3, 1988, revised February 9, 1989). The broad context of missile proliferation is examined in Janne E. Nolan, *Trappings of Power: Ballistic Missiles in the Third World* (Washington, D.C.: Brookings Institution, 1991).

2. At the beginning of 1990, ten countries had missile forces. The merger of North and South Yemen reduced the total by one. The Kuwaiti FROG-7 force was eliminated by the Iraqi invasion in August 1990.

3. These include the 1973 Arab-Israeli War, during which Syria launched an estimated twenty-five FROG-7 rockets and Egypt fired three Scud-B missiles and an unknown number of FROG-7 rockets at Israeli targets. In the course of the Iran-Iraq War, a total of more than 1,000 surface-to-surface missiles and rockets were fired, including almost 500 Scud and extended-range Scud missiles. (Iraq fired about 360 missiles, divided between 170 Scud-B and just under 190 Al-Hussein extended-range derivatives of the Scud. Starting in 1985, the Iranians responded by launching nearly 120 Scud-B missiles at Iraqi cities.) After the 1986 U.S. air attacks on Libya, the Libyans fired at least two Scud-B missiles at U.S. installations on the Italian island of Lampedusa in retaliation. The most important instance was during the 1991 Persian Gulf War, during which Iraq fired at least eighty-one missiles at Saudi Arabia and Israel, killing an estimated 31 people and injuring more than 400 others.

4. Unless otherwise noted, the information in this section is drawn from sources cited in note 1 or in one of two earlier studies by W. Seth Carus, "Missiles in the Middle East: A New Threat to Stability," *Policy Focus*, Washington Institute for Near East Policy, Research Memorandum no. 6, June 1988, and *Ballistic Missiles in the Third World: Threat and Response*, Washington Paper for Center for Strategic and International Studies (New York: Praeger, 1990).

5. The following account is based on W. Seth Carus and Joseph S. Bermudez, Jr., "Iran's Emerging Missile Forces," *Jane's Defence Weekly*, July 23, 1988, 126–131.

6. "Libya Wants CSS-2," *Flight International*, May 14, 1988, 14; and Arie Egozi, "Libya's Gadhafi Indicates Strong Interest in Chinese Ground to Ground Missiles," *Defense News*, June 13, 1988, 33. The *Defense News* article claims that a contract was signed, but the *Flight International* story indicates only that negotiations were taking place. Both stories come from Israeli sources.

7. John K. Cooley, *Libyan Sandstorm* (New York: Holt, Rinehart and Winston, 1982), 237–239.

8. *O Estado de Sao Paulo* (Portuguese), January 22, 1988, as translated by British Broadcasting Corporation, *Summary of World Broadcasts*, January 26, 1988, p. ME/0058/D/1; and by Foreign Broadcast Infor-

mation Service (FBIS), *Daily Report: Latin America*, January 25, 1988, 23.

9. During the last days of the Iran-Iraq War, President Hashemi-Rafsanjani, then speaker of the Iranian parliament and acting commander-in-chief of Iranian military forces, argued that "for us, missiles have a deterrent role." He believed that missiles were necessary "so that the very thought of an attack with missiles will be eliminated from our neighbor's minds." Interview on Tehran Television Service (Persian), March 28, 1988, as translated by FBIS, *Daily Report: Near East and South Asia*, March 29, 1988, 56–57.

10. Saudi Arabia's CSS-2 missiles obviously did not deter Iraq from attacking Saudi cities, and the Saudis recognized that retaliatory missile strikes against Iraq were not an option during the recent Persian Gulf War for both military and political reasons.

11. Most sources accept that Israel has the technology needed to produce a nuclear warhead sufficiently small to fit on a missile like the Jericho.

12. The INF agreement required the United States and the former Soviet Union to eliminate all ground-launched, surface-to-surface missiles with ranges of between 500 and 5,500 kilometers. The October 1991 Bush proposal, which was shortly followed by a proposal from Soviet President Mikhail Gorbachev, proposes the elimination of all ground- and sea-based short-range nuclear missiles. See, for instance, Fred Hiatt, "Gorbachev Pledges Wide-Ranging Nuclear Cuts," *Washington Post*, October 6, 1991, A1.

13. Barry Blechman, "Confidence-Building in the North Pacific: A Pragmatic Approach to Naval Arms Control," Peace Research Centre Working Paper 29 (Canberra: Australian National University, February 1988), 14.

14. UN General Assembly, "Report of the Secretary-General, Establishment of a Nuclear-Weapon-Free Zone in the Region of the Middle East," A/45/435, October 10, 1990, 41–42.

15. "Fact Sheet on the Middle East Arms Control Initiative, May 29, 1991" (Washington, D.C.: The White House Press Office), 1.

16. At least five systems of this type have been developed in the Middle East, including the Egyptian Saqr-80, with a range of 70 kilometers; Iran's Nazeat, a rocket with a range of 90 kilometers; the Iraqi version of the Ababil with a range of 100 kilometers and modified FROG-7 with a range of 90 kilometers, and Israel's MAR-350, which may achieve ranges estimated at 90 kilometers. Controls on systems

such as the SS-21 and Lance therefore would also require taking these new long-range artillery rockets into account. The sheer number of long-range artillery rockets and short-range ballistic missiles available in the region, however, may make it impossible to impose constraints on weapons with ranges of less than 100 kilometers.

17. The United States converted a version of its Harpoon antiship missile, the SLAM, into a land-attack missile. The modification makes use of off-the-shelf components, many of which could be available to countries in the Middle East. Similar modifications could be made to other antiship missiles already in Middle Eastern arsenals, including the Italian OTOMAT and the Chinese Silkworm.

18. The Israelis are known to have developed harassment drones, which essentially are low-speed cruise missiles for attacking radars and radio transmitters. Moreover, the Israelis have developed much of the technology needed to produce a land-attack cruise missile at least comparable with the SLAM.

19. The U.S. Army's Nike Hercules missile, which was designed with a secondary surface-to-surface role, was reverse engineered by South Korea in the 1980s to develop its first surface-to-surface missile, the NHK. Similarly, Taiwan also has given a secondary surface-to-surface role to the Tien Kung 2, a new surface-to-air missile similar in design to the U.S. Patriot. And the United States adapted the Patriot surface-to-air missile for use as a surface-to-surface missile during tests of the Assault Breaker deep attack concept as early as the 1970s.

There are examples of such conversions in the Middle East. The Iraqis claim to have developed surface-to-surface versions of Soviet-supplied SA-2 and SA-3 missiles. The SA-2 has a warhead weighing nearly 450 pounds, giving it a larger payload than Iraq's extended-range Scuds. It might be possible to do the same for the SA-5 missiles the Soviet Union supplied to Syria and Libya.

20. Max M. Kampelman and Edward C. Luck, "Ban Missiles in the Middle East," *Washington Post*, April 18, 1991, p. A21. The most complete discussion is contained in Kathleen C. Bailey, "Arms Control for the Middle East," *International Defense Review* (April 1991):311–314. Some of these ideas were first articulated in Kathleen Bailey, "Can Missile Proliferation Be Reversed?," *Orbis* (Winter 1991):13.

21. Although Iraq announced it had a missile with a range of 650 kilometers in August 1987, the claim was dismissed as propaganda.

22. Even under a total ban on certain types of missiles, it may be difficult to identify and locate medium-range missiles and their

launchers. In early 1990 three Warsaw Pact countries were discovered to have SS-23 missiles, a system banned under terms of the INF Treaty. According to the Soviet Union, the missiles were turned over to East Germany, Czechoslovakia, and Bulgaria prior to completion of the negotiations. Thus, for more than two years, several Warsaw Pact countries possessed a significant number of illicit missiles without the knowledge of the United States. Because few areas of the world received as much surveillance as eastern Europe, the time that was required to discover the presence of the SS-23 missiles is sobering.

23. One illustration of challenging verification problems relates to the U.S. Army's ATACMS missile system, believed to have a range of between 150 and 200 kilometers, depending on its warhead. The ATACMS is fired from the same MLRS launcher developed for a 30-kilometer range artillery rocket. Both weapons are transported and fired from closed pods, making it difficult to verify whether a launcher is equipped with a 30-kilometer or a 150-kilometer weapon.

24. It also might be relatively easy for countries in the Middle East to develop a missile capability in a country outside the region, if necessary, in order to evade arms control constraints. The process could work in the following manner: A Middle Eastern country would reach an agreement with a state in some other part of the world to provide missiles under specified circumstances. The Middle Eastern country might even send crews to the foreign supplier for training. The missiles could then be shipped to the region in the event of a crisis.

25. Michael R. Gordon, "U.S. Urges Talks on Missiles in Mideast," *New York Times,* December 27, 1988, p. A3. According to Gordon, the Pentagon vetoed this idea because of potential negative repercussions on U.S. negotiating positions in Europe.

26. Hirschfeld, "Mutual Security Short of Arms Control," 34–36.

27. The limitations on weapons deployments, however vital, are only one facet of a broader political accommodation made possible only after Egypt and Israel achieved a political understanding in the Camp David Accords.

5. Flowerree and Roberts, "Chemical Weapons Arms Control"

1. Testimony by Rear Admiral Thomas A. Brooks, director of U.S. Naval Intelligence, to the House Armed Services Committee, Subcommittee on Seapower, Strategic, and Critical Materials, March 7, 1991.

2. The discussion of the chemical weapons capabilities of individual countries draws heavily on Gordon M. Burck's and Charles C. Flowerree's *International Handbook on Chemical Weapons Proliferation* (New York: Greenwood Press with the Federation of American Scientists, 1991).

3. Don Oberdorfer and Ann Devroy, "State Department Calls Iraq's Figures on Weapons 'Short of Reality,' " *Washington Post*, April 30, 1991, p. A1.

4. Statement by Robert Galucci, deputy executive chairman of the Special Commission, at the Center for Strategic and International Studies, October 28, 1991.

5. Cited in "Iraq War Damage Estimates Vary," *Financial Times*, June 13, 1991, p. 1.

6. Saddam Hussein, comments in Spanish TV interview, FBIS, NES-90-250, December 28, 1990.

7. W. Andrew Terrill, "The Chemical Warfare Legacy of the Yemen War," *Comparative Strategy* 10, no. 2 (April–June 1991):109–119.

8. William Beecher, "Egypt Deploying Nerve Gas Weapons," *Washington Post*, June 6, 1976, p. 1; and "Egypt Seen Set to Use Nerve Gas," *Washington Post*, June 6, 1976, p. 14.

9. Julian Perry Robinson, "The Changing Status of Chemical and Biological Warfare: Recent Technical, Military and Political Developments," *SIPRI Yearbook 1982: World Armaments and Disarmament* (New York: Taylor & Francis, 1982), 336; and see E.E. Galal in *Pugwash Newsletter* 13, no. 4 (April 1976):198.

10. Robin Wright, "U.S. Leaks Word of Egypt Chemical Plant," *Los Angeles Times*, March 11, 1989, p. 9.

11. Reuters from Abu Dhabi, in "Arabs 'Need Chemical Weapons,' " *Independent*, July 28, 1988.

12. Thus, Egypt was strictly speaking in violation of the Geneva Protocol when it used chemical weapons against Yemen in the 1960s, even though the Yemen Arab Republic did not become a party until March 17, 1971.

13. CD/PV.459, April 21, 1988.

14. David Ottaway, "Mubarak, Bush Differ on Peace Talks," *Washington Post*, April 4, 1989, p. 14.

15. It should be noted, however, that a right to in-kind retaliation may have accrued to all parties to the Protocol. If the number of states (including the United States) taking that reservation is regarded as

sufficient, then the Protocol, as limited by that reservation, is the actual customary international law.

16. IRNA [Iranian News Agency], July 5, 1984, FBIS-SAS, July 6, 1984.

17. IRNA, May 27, 1985, FBIS-SAS, May 28, 1985.

18. Daniel Williams, "Israel Hopes to Deter Attack of Poison Gas," *Los Angeles Times,* October 9, 1988, pp. 1, 12–13.

19. Jerusalem domestic service in English, January 7, 1989, FBIS-NES, January 9, 1989.

20. *Jerusalem Post,* March 13, 1989, p. 1, FBIS-NES, March 15, 1989. Although the distinction is not recognized in the Geneva negotiations, some officials might see a difference between bulk agents and filled munitions, considering only the latter as "weapons."

21. Edward M. Spiers, *Chemical Warfare* (Urbana, Ill.: University of Illinois Press, 1986), 91, citing several histories in endnote 4-3. One source reports twenty-four mustard gas bombs dropped on a Libyan oasis in 1930. See Ronald Koven, "Nations Back a Chemical Weapons Ban," *Boston Globe,* January 12, 1989, p. 4.

22. JANA in Arabic, November 15, 1988, FBIS-NES, November 15, 1988.

23. Paris domestic service, January 8, 1989, JPRS-TAC-89-003, January 27, 1989. At the Paris Conference, the Libyan foreign minister said that Libya "has always respected the Geneva agreement [Protocol] on chemical weapons" (Paris domestic service, January 8, 1989, JPRS-TAC-89-003, January 27, 1989).

24. Voice of Greater Arab Homeland in Arabic, March 15, 1990, FBIS-NES, March 15, 1990.

25. "Arms Race 'Worsening,'" *Daily Telegraph,* December 28, 1987, p. 6.

26. Damascus domestic service in Arabic, January 8, 1989, JPRS-TAC-89-003, January 27, 1989.

27. The observers are allowed to comment on issues under negotiation but do not take part in the decision-making aspects of the drafting process. The observers also include a number of others from the region not suspected of possessing chemical weapons: Jordan, Kuwait, Oman, Qatar, and the United Arab Emirates.

28. See Brad Roberts, *Chemical Disarmament and International Security* (London: Brassey's for IISS, 1992); and *The Projected Chemical Weapons Convention: A Guide to the Negotiations in the Conference on*

Disarmament (New York and Geneva: UN Institute for Disarmament Research, 1990).

29. James A. Schear, "Combatting Chemical Weapons Proliferation: The Role of Assurances" (Washington, D.C.: Henry L. Stimson Center, April 1991). This quotation originally appeared in Ahmed Kamal, "The Chemical Weapons Convention: Some Particular Concerns of Developing Countries," *Chemical Weapons Convention Bulletin* (Washington, D.C.: Federation of American Scientists, May 1989).

30. For a review of the issues, see Lewis Dunn and James Schear, "Combatting Chemical Weapons Proliferation: The Role of Sanctions and Assurances," Occasional Paper 3 (Washington, D.C.: Henry L. Stimson Center, 1991).

31. Some examples of sanctions that might be applied to punish a violator of international norms established for chemical weapons include termination of selected chemical exports or imports, loss of import and export preferences, cut-off of economic aid, freeze on financial assets, bans on military sales and assistance, bans on technical training of violator's nationals, withdrawal of aircraft landing rights, and a cut-off of diplomatic relations.

32. "Chemical and Biological Weapons Proliferation," Executive Order 12375, November 16, 1990. In March 1991 the U.S. government imposed curbs on exports of fifty commonly used chemicals and the equipment that could turn them to military use. The rules require companies to get Commerce Department licenses for exports to specified countries including Israel, Kuwait, Saudi Arabia, Bahrain, the United Arab Emirates, Qatar, Egypt, and Syria. Exports to Iraq, of course, were still prohibited.

33. Dunn and Schear, "Combatting Chemical Weapons," 2–3, 12.

34. Nabil Fahmy, "The Security of Developing Countries and Chemical Disarmament," in *Chemical Disarmament and U.S. Security*, ed. Brad Roberts (Boulder, Colo.: Westview Press, forthcoming).

35. Report of the Secretary General of the UN, "Establishment of a Nuclear-Weapon-Free Zone in the Region of the Middle East," A/45/435, October 10, 1990, 35.

36. Ibid.

37. David Hoffman, "Shevardnadze Urges Nuclear-Free Zone in Middle East," *Washington Post*, December 12, 1990, p. A29.

38. Ibid.

39. This weakness was discussed at the September 1991 Review Conference of the Parties to the Treaty, the third such conference for

the treaty since it went into force in 1975. But an effective compliance regime for the BWC will have to await completion of the CWC, whose verification procedures, which are relevant to verification of a biological weapons ban, are still being elaborated at the Geneva negotiations.

40. For example, in former CIA director William Webster's February 6, 1989 testimony before Congress, he indicated that at least ten countries have offensive biological warfare programs. In open session, he noted that among these, some are in the Middle East and some are known sponsors of terrorism. *New York Times*, February 7, 1989, p. 1.

41. Statement by Mr. David Ben-Rafael, representative of Israel at the Amendment Conference of the States Parties to the Treaty Banning Nuclear Weapons Tests in the Atmosphere, in Outer Space and Under Water, New York, January 18, 1991.

42. James E. Goodby, "Transparency in the Middle East," *Arms Control Today* 21, no. 4 (May 1991).

43. Some analysts saw the INF Treaty as a chemical arms control measure even though it failed to even mention that type of munition. Because the treaty compelled both sides to allocate more scarce delivery systems to their most effective and reliable warheads, it is suggested that there may have been some turning away from chemical warheads by the Soviet Union and Warsaw Pact countries.

44. Stuart Auerbach, "19 Nations Back U.S. Plan for Chemical Arms Curbs," *Washington Post*, May 31, 1991, p. A1.

45. Dunn and Schear, "Combatting Chemical Weapons," 4.

United States Institute of Peace

The United States Institute of Peace is an independent, nonpartisan, federal institution created and funded by Congress to strengthen the nation's capacity to promote the peaceful resolution of international conflict. Established in 1984, the Institute has its origins in the tradition of American statesmanship, which seeks to limit international violence and to achieve a just peace based on freedom and human dignity. The Institute meets its congressional mandate to expand available knowledge about ways to achieve a more peaceful world through an array of programs, including grantmaking, a three-tiered fellowship program, research and studies projects, development of library resources, and a variety of citizen education activities. The Institute is governed by a fifteen-member Board of Directors, including four members ex officio from the executive branch of the federal government and eleven individuals appointed from outside federal service by the President of the United States and confirmed by the Senate.

Board of Directors